How to Focus an Evaluation

Brian M. Stecher
W. Alan Davis

Center for the Study of Evaluation
University of California, Los Angeles

SAGE PUBLICATIONS
The International Professional Publishers
Newbury Park   London   New Delhi

The second edition of the *Program Evaluation Kit* was developed at the Center for the Study of Evaluation, Graduate School of Education, University of California, Los Angeles.

The development of this second edition of the CSE *Program Evaluation Kit* was supported in part by a grant from the National Institute of Education, currently known as the Office of Educational Research and Improvement. However, the opinions expressed herein do not necessarily reflect the position or the policy of that agency and no official endorsement should be inferred.

The second edition of the *Program Evaluation Kit* is published and distributed by Sage Publications, Inc., of Newbury Park, California, under an exclusive agreement with the Regents of the University of California.

This is a substantially revised version of *How to Deal With Goals and Objectives* by Lynn Lyons Morris and Carol Taylor Fitz-Gibbon, Volume 2 in the first edition of the *Program Evaluation Kit*.

For information address:

SAGE Publications, Inc.
2455 Teller Road
Newbury Park, California 91320
E-mail: order@sagepub.com

SAGE Publications Ltd.
6 Bonhill Street
London EC2A 4PU
United Kingdom

SAGE Publications India Pvt. Ltd.
M-32 Market
Greater Kailash I
New Delhi 110 048 India

Printed in the United States of America

Library of Congress Cataloging-in-Publication Data

Stecher, Brian M.
　　　How to focus an evaluation / Brian M. Stecher, W. Alan Davis.
　　　　　p.　　cm.—(Program evaluation kit ; 2)
　　　Rev. ed. of: How to deal with goals and objectives / Lynn Lyons
Morris, Carol Taylor Fitz-Gibbon. c1978.
　　　Bibliography: p.
　　　Includes index.
　　　ISBN 0-8039-3127-1 (pbk.)
　　　1. Educational surveys. 2. Educational planning.　I. Davis, W.
Alan (William Alan)　II. Morris, Lynn Lyons.　How to deal with goals
and objectives.　III. Title.　IV. Series: Program evaluation kit
(2nd ed.) ; 2.
LB2823.S73　1987　　　　87-21759
379.1'54—dc19

96　97　98　99　00　01　02　21　20　19　18　17　16　15

Contents

Acknowledgments

The preparation of this second edition of the Center for the Study of Evaluation *Program Evaluation Kit* has been a challenging task, made possible only through the combined efforts of a number of individuals.

First and foremost, Drs. Lynn Lyons Morris and Carol Taylor Fitz-Gibbon, the authors and editor of the original Kit. Together, they authored all eight of the original volumes, an enormous undertaking that required incredible knowledge, dedication, persistence, and painstaking effort. Lynn also worked relentlessly as editor of the entire set. Having struggled through only a revision, I stand in great awe of Lynn's and Carol's enormous accomplishment. This second edition retains much of their work and obviously would not have been possible without them.

Thanks also are due to Gene V Glass, Ernie House, Michael Q. Patton, Carol Weiss, and Robert Boruch, who reviewed our plans and offered specific assistance in targeting needed revisions. The work would not have proceeded without Marvin C. Alkin, who planted the seeds for the second edition and collaborated very closely during the initial planning phases.

I would like to acknowledge especially the contribution and help of Michael Q. Patton. True to form, Michael was an excellent, utilization-focused formative evaluator for the final draft manuscript, carefully responding to our work and offering innumerable specific suggestions for its improvement. We have incorporated into the *Handbook* his framework for differentiating among kinds of evaluation studies (formative, summative, implementation, outcomes).

Many staff members at the Center for the Study of Evaluation contributed to the production of the Kit. The entire effort was supervised by Aeri Lee, able office manager at the Center. Katherine Fry, word processing expert, was able to accomplish incredible graphic feats for the *Handbook* and tirelessly labored on manuscript production and data transfer. Ruth Paysen, who was a major contributor to the production of the original Kit, also was a painstaking and dedicated proofreader for the second edition. Margie Franco, Tori Gouveia, and Katherine Lu also participated in the production effort.

Marie Freeman and Pamela Aschbacher, also from the Center, contributed their ideas, editorial skills, and endless examples. Carli

Rogers, of UCLA Contracts and Grants, was both caring and careful in her negotiations for us.

At Sage Publications, thanks to Sara McCune for her encouragement and to Mitch Allen for his nudging and patience.

And at the Center for the Study of Evaluation, the project surely would not have been possible without Eva L. Baker, Director. Eva is a continuing source of encouragement, ideas, support, fun, and friendship.

—Joan L. Herman
Center for the Study of Evaluation
University of California, Los Angeles

Foreword

Professional notions about program evaluation have grown considerably in recent years. Before 1960, in most social service areas evaluation generally entailed fact-finding missions by visiting teams of experts. In education the reporting of test scores also was common. In the 1960s experimental research methods were widely applied to determine the effectiveness of social programs, and several other conceptual models of evaluation were developed. Today the evaluator can draw upon a rich repertoire of approaches.

The broad range of models available to the modern evaluator presented a difficult choice in writing this guide. An overly broad approach, giving full consideration to several models of evaluation, might prove to be too abstract or complex to provide practical assistance. A narrow approach which presupposed a single model could provide practical guidance at the risk of perpetuating evaluation practices which were neither useful nor appropriate. We decided to err on the broad side and present a handful of different approaches to evaluation.

We will discuss these five approaches to evaluation without making comparative judgments, leaving it to the reader to select among them as appropriate. Our decision to concentrate on 'focusing' an evaluation rather than applying a specific set of guidelines reflects our assumption that an evaluator should approach an evaluation project from an open perspective and customize the process by selecting from a broad array of options. Focusing occurs gradually as the evaluator develops an understanding of the program, the expectations of the sponsor and other concerned parties, the evaluator's own assumptions, and the constraints of the situation. We hope that this book will provide practical guidance in the process.

Organization of This Book

This book is divided into four chapters that describe the focusing process in roughly chronological order. Since the process itself is not always linear (in fact, it can be quite convoluted), a strictly sequential presentation is not realistic. However, we have tried to simplify matters and present information in a fairly logical order. Chapter 1 presents a simple model of the process of focusing an evaluation. While there is no fixed series of steps that can be followed in a routine manner to arrive at a good basis for every evaluation, there are a number of elements that are present whenever a client and an evaluator get together to discuss a project. Understanding these elements will make you more effective at focusing an evaluation. The elements to be discussed are the *existing beliefs and expectations* of the sponsor and the evaluator, the process of *gathering information*, and the process of *formulating a plan* for the evaluation. Chapter 1 provides the common language and structure to be explicated in the rest of the book.

Chapter 2 explores the beliefs and expectations that all parties bring to the focusing process. Particular attention is given to the underlying concept of evaluation that each party possesses. Five different perspectives on the evaluation process will be presented: the experimental approach, the goal-oriented approach, the decision-focused approach, the user-oriented approach, and the responsive approach. Since the evaluator's point of view about evaluation affects all of his or her interactions, you will be asked to consider your own perspective on evaluation.

Chapter 3 discusses the process of gathering information. What do you need to know to develop an effective strategy for conducting an evaluation? What questions do you ask to obtain this information? This chapter will explore these basic questions from each of the five different evaluation perspectives.

Chapter 4 explains how to finish the focusing process by developing an evaluation plan. Because much of this process takes place in the evaluator's mind, this is one of the most difficult topics to discuss. The chapter includes a description of the desired outcome of the focusing process—the evaluation plan—and provides guidelines to illustrate what a reasonably well-focused plan might look like. Then it presents an approach for organizing information that facilitates the development of a viable evaluation plan.

We suggest that you follow the chapters in order. The beginning chapters establish the framework and define terminology that will be used extensively in the later chapters.

Author's Acknowledgment

We would like to express our sincere appreciation to Marvin C. Alkin, who first proposed this book and helped us to focus our own thinking about these issues. We also would like to thank Michael Patton, who reviewed the manuscript and offered useful suggestions.

Chapter 1
Thinking About the Focusing Process

First steps have added importance in any journey; they foretell the direction of the trip, and they establish a tone or style that carries through the rest of the way. A similar observation can be made about evaluation. The initial discussions between evaluator and sponsor usually establish the goals that will guide the endeavor, the type of procedures that will be used, and the style of interaction that will characterize the collaboration. The purpose of this book is to explain how to work collaboratively to establish a reasonable framework for an evaluation. Developing this framework is what we refer to as "focusing the evaluation."

The word "focus" is used to describe this process because it suggests sharpening an image and bringing clarity to a situation. When you focus an evaluation, you sharpen your understanding of the needs and wishes of program personnel and of sponsors and clarify their understanding of your experience and capabilities. In addition, you formulate the ground rules that will apply to the evaluation and select the issues that will be addressed. This process involves sharing information about the program or the sponsor's needs and the evaluator's expertise, specifying a set of questions or issues to be addressed by the evaluation, and agreeing upon the general approach that will be used in information-gathering and analysis. This book is designed to make you aware of the elements that are involved in this process and to show you how to go about arriving at a good basis for conducting an evaluation.

Imagine the following situation. You are about to meet the director of a local social service agency for the first time, knowing only that the agency wants to conduct an evaluation. You are escorted into the office and are greeted cordially. The director explains that you were very highly recommended by a trusted colleague; you respond with proper humility. Then there is a long pause. The director looks at you; you look back. The stage is set, but how does the drama unfold?

In the ideal scenario, this is the start of a fruitful discussion in which the director describes the program, the issues that are important to all interested parties, and the questions that need to be answered. You, in turn, explain your approach to evaluation, the way you like to operate, and some of the expertise you can bring to this investigation. Together you narrow the discussion to a few key issues that can be addressed in a meaningful way, identify strategies for answering the questions, and agree on general guidelines for the evaluation.

Of course, this process may take many discussions. It may take place in face-to-face meetings, in conversations over the telephone, or in written correspondence. Occasionally, if you and a potential sponsor differ dramatically concerning the goals and procedures of the evaluation, you may choose not to work together at all. Yet regardless of the form of the negotiations or their outcome, an effective evaluator needs to understand how to go about focusing an evaluation in a clear manner. Only in this way will the sponsor and the evaluator understand what they hope to accomplish and what the fruits of a collaborative effort are likely to be. These negotiations are the subject of this book.

Of course, no book can tell you everything you need to know. There is no magic five-step procedure for focusing an evaluation. Evaluators' skills and points of view vary, as do the needs and temperaments of program staff and other concerned parties. So there is no exact formula that will work in every situation. The goal of this book is to help you develop the skills you will need to build a good foundation—a shared understanding of the evaluation's purposes and approach—which is a necessary condition for an effective collaboration.

Of course, there is much to be done after an evaluation has been focused. Data collection, data analysis, and the communication of evaluation findings usually occupy the lion's share of an evaluator's time. These activities are covered by other books in the *Program Evaluation Kit*.

A Framework for Focusing an Evaluation

Focusing an evaluation is a complex task. It involves negotiations between people who do not always share the same beliefs and attitudes, who do not possess the same information about the topics they are discussing, and who do not place equal value on the same potential outcomes. Moreover, it is a human interaction, and, like all human interactions, it is full of subtleties and subject to infinite variation. We acknowledge up front that such complexity and variation exists when focusing an evaluation, and so accept the need for simplification. It would be impossible in a brief book such as this to account for every possible situation or provide for every combination of factors. Instead, we have simplified the process into four general elements. Certainly something is lost in this simplification, but something is gained also. The framework that emerges is a better tool for communicating our ideas about evaluation and teaching you useful skills. After you have completed this book and begun to work with sponsors and other concerned individuals, you will find that it is easy to accommodate the subtleties and variations that we have omitted.

Another simplification we have made is to talk as if the evaluation is being conducted for a particular individual—referred to as "the client." The focusing process is described as if it were a one-to-one dialogue or discussion among two or three individuals. While such situations occur, the reader must remember to think of the "client" in broader terms. An evaluation may be conducted on behalf of a program officer from a funding agency, the project director, the board of directors, the professional staff, the program participants, concerned citizens and community members, or society in general. The evaluator may interact directly with one or all of these groups. The generic term "client" will be used to simplify the discussion, but it should be understood to include all possible sponsors and interested parties. In Chapter 4 we discuss the problem of working with such groups.

Similarly, the evaluator must guard against the tendency to limit his or her contact to a narrow range of program or agency personnel. One of evaluation's major failings in the 1960s was the fact that evaluation findings were not used in significant ways. This lack of utilization can be traced, in part, to the limited involvement of concerned individuals and people who had a stake in program outcomes.

Elements of the Focusing Process

If you ask evaluators about focusing an evaluation, they usually think of identifying particular goals and objectives and stipulating specific evaluation questions. If you ask them how the process occurs, they are less certain, but will probably mention something about an exchange of information between the evaluator and the client. For example, the evaluator asks about the program's goals and objectives, and the client explains the program's anticipated outcomes. From there it is easy for the evaluator to set up a timetable for administering tests to measure attainment of the objectives. *Voila*, the plan for the evaluation emerges!

As we see it, the process is much more complex. In fact, it begins *before* the client and evaluator ever meet. Both come to the initial meeting with preconceived ideas about evaluation and expectations for what might be accomplished. Even after they meet they do more than merely identify program goals and establish testing plans. Both parties try to learn more about the needs and capabilities of the other and the benefits that can accrue to the program from an evaluation. A great deal of information is shared during this process. Only after discussing a wide variety of options do they begin to establish priorities and identify a limited number of targets. Finally, general guidelines are agreed upon that constitute a plan for the evaluation.

To understand this process better, think about what might occur at the first meeting between an evaluator and a new client. For example, imagine that the client is the program director of a local agency. The evaluator is someone recommended by a mutual acquaintance. In the best of all possible worlds, the meeting will give the two individuals an opportunity to meet each other, discuss the issues, and reach an agreement on a general plan to evaluate the program. But how does that actually occur?

We think there are three distinct elements in the focusing process:

- existing beliefs and expectations;
- gathering information; and
- formulating an evaluation plan.

All three of these components are present whenever an evaluation is planned.

Though there is a logical sequence to these elements, we prefer not to refer to them as "steps." In reality the discussions can move back and forth many times between formulating preliminary plans and sharing more information before a final strategy is identified. In fact, one may develop a specific evaluation plan only to discover that some critical information was lacking, making it necessary to initiate new discussions. Seldom does everything occur in a nice orderly sequence. Yet the three elements are always present, and it is important to understand how they interact to produce a viable evaluation plan. The following sections will describe the elements of this process in greater detail.

Existing Beliefs and Expectations

In a sense, the focusing process begins before the client and evaluator meet. Each person comes to the meeting with beliefs about evaluation and expectations for the collaboration. Each evaluator has his or her own concept of evaluation. Is evaluation a question of control groups and statistical analyses? Is it an attempt to assess the attainment of stated goals and objectives? Or is it geared toward providing information related to specific program decisions?

Many answers are possible because many different approaches to evaluation exist. If you were to ask prominent scholars in the field to define the term "evaluation," to describe its goals, and to indicate the procedures they would use to conduct an evaluation, you would get many different answers. We use the term "evaluation approach" to signify a point of view about the proper way to conduct an evaluation. Each approach embodies a certain set of assumptions about what evaluation should accomplish, what kinds of activities are appropriate, what sorts of results will be produced, and how they will be communicated.

There are many evaluation approaches. Probably the most familiar is one we call the "experimental approach." As will be explained in the following chapter, evaluators who adopt an experimental approach try to apply the principles of experimental design to evaluation questions. They try to draw generalizable conclusions about a program in the way a researcher might approach an experimental study. Program effects are isolated by using control groups and statistical tests, and the evaluation itself is structured to be as scientifically rigorous as possible. Other approaches emphasize different elements and use different procedures.

Whether you realize it or not, you too probably have a point of view about evaluation. When a client asks you for advice, you are likely to suggest alternatives that reflect your own approach. If you feel strongly about the efficacy of a particular point of view, you may try to convince the client that this is the right framework to use. If you are unfamiliar with certain approaches it is doubtful that you will analyze the situation from these perspectives or suggest courses of action that reflect these points of view. Furthermore, two evaluators with different approaches to evaluation will respond differently to the same client. The evaluation that results from one collaboration may be focused entirely differently than the evaluation that results from the other.

The client, too, enters the meeting with expectations about evaluation. For example, for many clients evaluation is synonymous with testing, particularly with pretest/posttest comparisons and other measures of achievement gain over time. Not all clients share this viewpoint—some have had experience with other types of evaluation—but many conceive of evaluation in this way. In addition, the client also enters the meeting with program-related concerns that he or she hopes will be solved by the evaluation. These concerns may derive from problems that have arisen in the project or from requirements of a funding source. Whatever their basis, such concerns color the way the client presents information, responds to questions from the evaluator, and judges the competence of the evaluator and the meaningfulness of what is said. Any ideas or suggestions offered by the evaluator will be interpreted by the client in light of his or her needs and expectations.

These pre-existing conditions will be described in greater detail in Chapter 2. For now, you should recognize that both evaluator and client have preconceived ideas and expectations about evaluation that will affect their collaboration. These constitute the first element in the focusing process.

Gathering Information

Another element in the focusing process is information-gathering. Both the evaluator and the client have a lot to learn. The evaluator must become familiar with the program, the client's needs and expectations for the evaluation, the individuals and groups who need to be included, and the limitations imposed on the evaluation by time, resources, and other constraints. The client wants to know about the evaluator's ability and the potential of evaluation to provide assistance.

There are general pieces of information the evaluator will need to know about almost any program. The additional questions you ask will depend upon the specific program you are discussing and the circumstances under which the evaluation will be conducted.

First, you will want a description of the program. Who are the program participants? What sort of services are provided? What are the goals of the program and how is their attainment measured? How many staff members are involved? What is the schedule of activities? How many sites are involved? You will need to obtain a fairly clear picture of how the program operates. Such descriptive details are likely to be important as you think about possible evaluation strategies.

Second, you will want to find out about the client's concerns. Why is an evaluation being considered? How are the results of the evaluation likely to be used? Why has the agency contacted an outside evaluator? This information is very important. Not only does it provide the starting point for formulating tentative solutions to the client's problems, it also tells you a great deal about the client's understanding and conception of evaluation. Moreover, you will learn how well they have formulated their concerns and how realistic their goals may be.

The third issue you may want to address in the information-gathering phase is whether there are other individuals or groups who are likely to have a stake in the outcome of the evaluation. Initial meetings usually take place among a small group of people, possibly just the program director or sponsor and the evaluator. It is very important to know who else will have an interest in the results of the evaluation. For one thing, you may want to gather information from other individuals or groups before formulating an evaluation strategy. You will be able to produce a more meaningful plan if you have all the relevant information. It is also important to know which parties are interested in the results of this information, because these people are likely to make their presence known during the course of the evaluation. You will want to consider whether it is important to consult with representatives of other constituencies.

Finally, evaluators will usually probe to discover what resources can be committed to evaluation and what constraints exist that might limit the scope of the endeavor. The resource question is a delicate one. Though some clients will have a precise budget in mind at this stage in negotiations, others will make final budget decisions based upon their discussions with the evaluator and the information that is provided about the cost and benefits of various alternatives. At this point you need only general guidelines to help you organize your thinking.

Constraints are an equally important concern. You will need to know about limitations that might be imposed by scheduling considerations, natural project cycles for the delivery of services, access to clients, and so forth. As you begin to formulate possible strategies, you will need to check that all necessary conditions exist for carrying out the activities you are considering.

At the same time the evaluator is probing to learn more about the program, the client is also trying to gather information. The client's concerns focus on the knowledge and capabilities of the evaluator, the value and limitations of evaluation for meeting local needs, and the types of procedures that will be carried out to conduct the evaluation. As evaluator, you will need to provide answers to these questions.

Formulating an Evaluation Plan

As you learn about the program and the client's concerns, you begin to think about ways to provide useful evaluation services. This process involves clarifying the questions raised by the client and trying to discern the relative importance of each inquiry, formulating strategies to gather data relating to these questions, and estimating the cost and feasibility of these alternatives. This is usually an interactive process that leads to the formulation of an evaluation plan.

Exactly what is an evaluation plan? When we speak of such a plan, we are referring to a general agreement between evaluator and client that clarifies key issues concerning the evaluation. The plan is usually preliminary to a signed agreement. It will probably be a verbal understanding rather than a written one. At a minimum, a useful evaluation plan will clarify three things: evaluation questions, procedures, and costs.

Questions may be stated in very specific terms: Do students achieve greater gains in reading comprehension under Program A than Program B? Did the program meet its goals of training 10% of the food service workers in the community in CPR techniques? Or they may be more broad statements of issues to be explored: What are the consequences of eliminating school librarians? Finally, they may be only general concerns: What is happening to school morale? Why are people so unhappy with the job training programs provided in community adult centers? In any case, you and the client should have a clear understanding of what problems the evaluation will investigate.

Second, you should clarify the procedures that will be used to carry out the study. Are you going to administer questionnaires? Will each client be expected to take a two-hour examination? Will you be visiting homes, observing workroom behaviors, chatting informally with teachers during their free periods? Data collection procedures may vary widely, and they will impose differing demands on program participants. Therefore, you should discuss the kinds of activities you are likely to undertake, the resources the client will provide, and the duration of the process.

Third, you should agree upon the general cost of the evaluation. You should try to "guesstimate" the amount of money that will be needed to carry out the activities that have been discussed. Choices among alternatives may depend on the relative costs of each operation, so you may need to estimate the cost of each component. A detailed budget with exact cost figures can be supplied later, but you should both agree at this time on the general level of funding that will be needed.

As you begin to formulate plans for an evaluation, you must always be conscious of how well you are meeting the client's needs. Occasionally differences between evaluator and client are so great that the client may be better served by a different evaluator.

Summary

This chapter outlines a model for focusing an evaluation. The model serves as an illustrative tool for talking about the procedures you might follow in working with clients. In general, the evaluator-client interaction will involve three elements: the existing beliefs and expectations of the evaluator and the client, the process of gathering information, and the process of formulating an evaluation plan. The following chapters will discuss each of these steps in detail.

Chapter 2
Thinking About Client Concerns and Evaluation Approaches

Evaluations are formulated by people, and each person approaches an evaluation with his or her own beliefs and expectations. The ability of a client and evaluator to agree upon a strategy for an evaluation depends, in part, on the concerns and attitudes they bring with them when they meet to discuss an evaluation. This chapter begins with an exploration of the client's expectations. Two questions are particularly important: What might motivate a client to seek the assistance of an evaluator? How will these factors affect the way the client approaches the collaboration? Following this discussion, the chapter examines the evaluator's mind-set. Five different approaches to evaluation will be described and their implications for the process of focusing an evaluation will be discussed.

Client Needs and Expectations

Why do program directors or sponsors consult evaluators? Since administrators have contact with the program on a regular basis, it would seem that they should be able to make accurate judgments about its success without relying on an external consultant. While most experienced administrators can estimate the effectiveness of their program fairly accurately, they realize that such judgments are subjective and can be improved through more systematic information-gathering. A desire for accurate measurement of program accomplishments prompts many program directors to consult specialists.

Moreover, as programs grow larger administrators find themselves further removed from "the action," relying more on communication from intermediate staff. This adds an additional filter to the information and reduces its objectivity. By systematically gathering data it becomes possible to make more accurate judgments about the program's accomplishments. Some of this can be done by program staff using existing records and documents. However, an outside expert (such as an evaluator) can often improve the process and assist in the development of more meaningful measurements.

Government mandates are another major reason that evaluations are conducted. Particularly in the field of education, legal requirements for program monitoring and assessment have been a significant impetus to evaluation. Federal regulations requiring evaluations were enacted in the 1960s to provide an independent measure of accountability that could be used to assess the impact of major federal expenditures on education. Similar regulations requiring independent evaluations were added to other government-sponsored social programs thereafter. Evaluation became the norm for most publicly funded social programs in the 1970s, and such legal mandates remain a strong impetus for current evaluation work.

Even in the absence of legal requirements, program advisory groups and administrators may desire accurate assessment of their program. They may want such information for a host of reasons: to support new funding initiatives, to improve program operations, or to enhance public relations. By hiring an evaluator who can gather relevant information in an unbiased manner, advisory boards and program staff can gain a degree of understanding about what is taking place in their program that could not usually be obtained through existing channels. For these reasons, and others, many administrators call upon evaluators to provide information to illuminate program-related issues and concerns.

These portrayals tell us something about the attitudes and expectations a client may bring to the first meeting with an evaluator. They provide some basis for anticipating what different clients are likely to want and how they are likely to interact with an evaluator.

One noteworthy distinction is between clients who are responding only to requirements and those who have a personal interest in the evaluation. As noted above, some program administrators are motivated almost entirely by legal mandates. They contact an evaluator because the funding agency requires it, but they have little personal stake or interest in the information that will be provided. They may care only that the funding source is satisfied. For example, a client may desire nothing more from an evaluator than a "clean bill of health" at minimum cost. Or a program may routinely collect all required information and need an evaluator only to attest to its accuracy. In such circumstances it may be possible for a creative evaluator to show the client how the process of evaluation can offer additional benefits, but not always. Instead, you may find little enthusiasm for or commitment to evaluation. In contrast, many clients seek out an evaluator because they have genuine concerns about the program and want assistance in providing information for program improvement. Even where evaluation is required, mandates may be flexible enough to allow concerned program staff to commission an evaluation that is meaningful to them as well as to the funding agency. In these circumstances, the evaluator is likely to find both interest and enthusiasm for the evaluation, which will make the focusing process more constructive.

Another important difference among clients is how well developed their questions and concerns are. Most clients who are not simply responding to narrow legal requirements will fit into one of three groups: (1) They may have clearly stated goals and objectives, and desire assistance to determine if these objectives are being met; (2) they may have questions about the program and want outside help in findings answers; or (3) they may only be able to articulate general concerns and need someone who can help them clarify and focus their thinking.

These three types of clients are easy to identify. The language of goals and objectives is fairly common among program administrators, and anyone who is really concerned about the attainment of program goals is likely to be quite direct about it. For example, a client may state quite specifically, "70% of our patients are supposed to be symptom-free for six months following treatment, and we want to find out if that is true." Similarly, those who have specific questions in mind will offer them for your consideration: "What we really want to know is whether we should switch from peer tutoring to computer-assisted instruction?" The third group represents the greatest challenge, for they often have difficulty stating their concerns in specific terms. They are more likely to speak about general issues. "Things are not going well among the professional staff, and I think it's affecting the clients."

These are examples of the three kinds of questions that might be posed by a client. Of course, you do not necessarily have to propose an evaluation that is identical in style and scope to the format the client has presented. Part of your role may be to draw out larger concerns and help the client clarify the issues that are most important. In any event, it will help to be aware of the three general types of inquiries you are likely to receive.

Finally, it is useful to realize that clients may have specific ideas about what evaluation means and how an evaluation is supposed to be conducted. For example, many clients will have preconceived notions about what you are supposed to measure. In education, most program administrators think of evaluation in terms of test scores. In fact, if you were to ask a hundred school program directors at random to explain how they would evaluate their program, the vast majority would suggest that the primary indicator of success should be students' growth in achievement based on the difference between pretest and posttest scores. In other fields, there are other traditional indices that are used frequently to measure success. In the criminal justice system it may be recidivism rates. In employment training programs it may be 60-day or 90-day retention rates. In almost every social program area experienced administrators will have some preconceived idea of what an evaluation is supposed to measure. Whether appropriate or not, ideas about these traditional indices act as a force to limit the discussion between evaluator and client.

Unfortunately, many program administrators also have preconceived ideas that evaluation is an intrusive activity. Clients who are acting on the basis of legal mandates are particularly likely to think of evaluation as something that is done *to* them and not something that has any value *for* them. Such experiences have been widely shared, and many administrators approach evaluation with some trepidation. As a result, part of your job in your initial meeting may be an educational one. You may need to illustrate ways in which evaluation can have more meaningful results for local program staff and participants.

As you prepare for your initial meeting, you should realize that the client has contacted you for a reason, and he or she will come into the meeting with certain needs or questions and with certain attitudes toward evaluation. All these client variables will affect the exchange that takes place. How you act in this initial meeting will also depend upon your own style and your own beliefs about evaluation. These beliefs are the subject of the next discussion.

Evaluation Approaches

The previous discussion was qualified with phrases such as "depending on your approach to evaluation" or "your beliefs about evaluation will affect the way you respond." These qualifications were necessary because there is no single, agreed upon definition for evaluation. Neither is there a single set of acceptable procedures that one follows in carrying out an evaluation study. Instead, there are a number of different conceptions about what evaluation means and how it should be done. We call these "evaluation approaches," and we use the term to indicate a coherent set of ideas about what an evaluation should accomplish and how it should be carried out—in other words, the goals and procedures of evaluation.

In the following sections five different approaches to evaluation will be described. Each has evolved as a way to provide useful information under different sets of circumstances. All share at least one important property: the desire to provide information that is meaningful to the client. Yet each interprets meaningfulness in a slightly different manner and places greater or lesser emphasis on differing aspects of data collection, analysis, and reporting.

The earliest modern evaluations were research studies in which the principles of academic research—experimental design, control groups, and the like—were applied to social programs. Many of these evaluation research activities provided important information for national policy-makers. Unfortunately, much of the evaluation performed according to this model was not very useful for the local program staff or the clients themselves.

Over time, educational researchers began to reconceive of evaluation in ways that were sensitive to other issues and were more relevant to local concerns. In the 1970s, many different conceptions of evaluation were formulated. Some focused on clarifying goals and objectives, others focused on the decision-making context and the relevance of information to key decisions. More recently, new theories of evaluation have been formulated that emphasize other factors, including the users of information and the human variables that enter into program actions. Some researchers have forsaken traditional quantitative approaches and embraced more naturalistic methods. These scholars recognize that actions have different meanings to different people, and believe that a program can only be understood from multiple perspectives representing different audiences.

The evaluator in the 1980s can paint with a palette of many colors. While few people embrace all approaches, most draw upon ideas from many while emphasizing one perspective that seems the best. Some themes are relevant to all approaches. All evaluators should strive to establish good rapport with clients and all would be wise to attend to organizational factors and political influences that affect clients (though these are issues of special concern to user-focused evaluators). You will have to decide which approaches are most meaningful for you. In the following sections we describe five approaches, placing particular emphasis on the impact of that perspective on the focusing process.

The Experimental Approach

By "the experimental approach" we mean an orientation toward evaluation that seeks to apply the principles of experimental science to the domain of social program evaluation. This approach is derived from the long tradition of controlled experimentation that marks most academic research. The goal of the experimental evaluator is to derive generalizable conclusions about the impact of a particular program by controlling extraneous factors and isolating program influences. The evaluator strives to apply the scientific method as much as possible.

An evaluator who adopts the experimental approach develops an evaluation the same way a scholar plans a research study. This includes establishing a clearly defined intervention, setting up a controlled situation in which some subjects receive the treatment while others do not, and comparing the performance of these groups to determine the impact of the program. The evaluator uses the basic techniques of experimental design—randomization, control groups, and longitudinal analyses—to draw conclusions about the impact of the treatment.

Of course, one can rarely conduct rigidly controlled experiments in real-world settings. The strict requirements of scientific research have to be adapted to the reality of the program setting. For example, it is often impossible to assign subjects randomly to treatment and control groups, though this is a fundamental requirement of most experimental designs. Under such circumstances the experimental evaluator would still strive to achieve as much control as possible through quasi-experimental designs and might use advanced statistical techniques—such as analysis of covariance—to adjust for differences that cannot be controlled in the program setting.

One way to characterize different approaches to evaluation in concise terms is to think about the main emphasis of each approach. In the case of the experimental approach, the main emphasis is on objective, generalizable answers to program-related questions. The evaluator who adopts this approach does so in the belief that the most important element of an evaluation is the technical validity of its conclusions.

The strengths of the experimental approach are its emphasis on objectivity and the generalizability of the conclusions reached using controlled experimentation techniques. These features give experimental evaluations high credibility for many program administrators and decision makers. This type of evaluation often finds an attentive audience among policymakers, who have to establish program guidelines and regulations.

The weaknesses of the approach include the difficulty of establishing controlled conditions in the real world in which most social programs operate, and its lack of sensitivity to the subtleties and complexities of human interactions. Experimental evaluations often tend to reduce complex influences to simple causal patterns.

Implications for focusing the evaluation. Adopting the experimental point of view (or any of the other approaches to evaluation) affects the way the evaluator interacts with clients and conducts the evaluation. In an experimental evaluation, the evaluator's major role is to be an objective third party who applies principles of research design to a given situation to produce unassailable information about program impact. In evaluation situations that demand an experimental study, the evaluator usually adopts the role of "research expert." Rarely will clients understand the requirements of the research design, the importance of randomization, the need for consistency across program groups, and so on. The evaluator possesses this knowledge, so it becomes the evaluator's job to reconcile the realities of the program with the demands of the research model. The evaluator strives to achieve as rigorous a study as possible within the constraints of the program setting.

How does this affect interactions between evaluator and client? The evaluator becomes a voice for planning and organization in order to maintain strict adherence to experimental rules. To maintain objectivity and independence, the evaluator strives *not* to be influenced by the beliefs, feelings, or desires of the program participants or staff. Moreover, much of the terminology and procedures of experimental research are foreign to program participants, so there may be additional psychological distance between program staff and evaluator. All of these factors act to heighten the evaluator's role as an external agent.

While the experimental approach emphasizes independence and objectivity, we do not mean to suggest that the evaluator is not friendly, personable, or cooperative. Quite the contrary, regardless of which approach one adopts, it is important to establish a good, positive rapport with the clients. This allows better communication and increases the likelihood that the evaluation will focus on relevant outcomes or questions and will be useful to the clients.

The reader who is interested in learning more about evaluation from this perspective is directed to the work of Campbell and Stanley (1966) and Rossi and Freeman (1982).

Example: The Experimental Approach

Belinda Dwyer works as a program analyst for the Office of Conservation in a midwestern state. One of the office's major projects is to increase residential energy conservation in the state, and they have experimented with a number of programs to accomplish this. One approach involves including conservation tips with each residential energy bill sent out by the local utility company. Another involves unsolicited telephone calls to residences to provide information about energy conservation in the home. These two projects are being considered for expansion on a statewide basis, and Belinda has been asked to conduct an evaluation to determine which is the more effective.

Belinda had been trained as a researcher and sees this as a good opportunity to use some of her skills. She develops a variation of the standard pretest/posttest, control group design to compare the impact of the two programs on energy use. First, a community that represents a typical cross section of the state is identified and a random sample of 1,000 residences is selected. Prior electricity, water, and gas consumption data for a six-month period are obtained for each residence from archives maintained by the utility companies. Each household is randomly assigned to one of three groups: a telephone group, an information mailing group, and a control group. For the next three months, households in the telephone group receive unsolicited calls with information about home energy conservation like those that had been tried out in the earlier experiment. Households in the informational mailing group receive enclosures with their utility bills offering home conservation ideas. Finally, households in the control group receive no additional information.

Energy use for all three groups is charted during the three months of the experiment and for three months thereafter. If the conservation programs are effective, there should be clear differences between the two treatment groups and the control group.

After six months Belinda reviews the data. Both treatment groups show a decline in the amount of electricity and gas consumed during the experiment, though neither shows any significant change in the amount of water consumption. There is little difference between the two groups. The group that received the phone calls shows a slightly greater decrease in the use of gas and electricity than the group that received the informational handouts in the mail; however, the difference is not statistically significant. As a result, Belinda writes a report to the director of the office concluding that both approaches are effective in bringing about a decrease in energy consumption. Neither appears to be better than the other. The director, of course, may consider additional factors in making his decision.

The Goal-Oriented Approach

One logical way to plan a program is to identify a specific set of goals and objectives and organize program activities to achieve them. A parallel to this systematic program development process will be found in the goal-oriented approach to evaluation. The goal-oriented approach uses program-specific goals and objectives as the criteria for determining success. The evaluator tries to measure the extent to which goals are attained and specific objectives are accomplished.

This approach to evaluation is a natural outgrowth of a very practical model for program design and development. This model encourages program developers to clarify the relationships between specific activities or services that are offered and particular results or outcomes that are to be achieved. Not only do staff need to clarify the links between activities and outcomes, they also must stipulate the desired results—the objectives—in clearly stated, measurable terms. In this way there are logical connections between activities, outcomes, and the procedures for measuring results.

Unfortunately, not all programs are planned in this manner, so not all programs have clearly stated goals and objectives. As a result, the goal-oriented evaluator may spend considerable time helping clients clarify their objectives and illuminate the links between goals and activities. When this is accomplished the evaluation task becomes much simpler.

When evaluators talk about goals and objectives most clients think in terms of outcomes. However, programs can also have procedural goals. The goal-oriented evaluator also can help clients clarify their implementation plans and identify process objectives that reflect the program's ability to carry out activities according to plan.

Once goals and objectives have been clarified, the evaluator's task is to determine the degree to which goals are attained. Various kinds of measurements will be used to accomplish this task, depending on the specific objectives to be assessed. The results of the evaluation will contain a description of the status of all program goals. In this way, success is measured in terms of program-specific criteria rather than comparisons with control groups or other programs. To the goal-oriented evaluator generalizability of conclusions is less important than program-relatedness.

Of course, the procedures that are used to measure the attainment of goals and objectives are chosen to be as rigorous as possible. A goal-oriented evaluator wants to have confidence that the results he or she reports are accurate. Thus the goal-oriented evaluator uses the most accurate measurement strategies he or she can devise, and relies upon modern statistical analysis when it is appropriate.

The strengths of the goal-oriented approach are its concern with the clear delineation of logical relationships between objectives and activities and its emphasis on elements that are important to the program. It encourages involved individuals to focus on specific elements that are meaningful to them. However, in so doing the goal-oriented evaluation may miss important unintended consequences. This potential narrowness and the possibility of overlooking important issues are the chief weaknesses of this approach.

Implications for focusing the evaluation. If you adopt an approach to evaluation that emphasizes the clear statement and measurement of program objectives, then this will affect the way you interact with your clients. Because the process of clarifying goals is highly interactive, the goal-oriented evaluator usually does not maintain the degree of independence that is characteristic of the experimental evaluator. The evaluator and the program staff meet, discuss, and revise the statements of outcomes to make them both meaningful and measurable. The evaluator acts as a collaborator, helping program staff to state their expectations in clear, concrete terms. The role adopted by the goal-oriented evaluator might be described best as a "mentor," working closely with program staff to help them clarify their thinking about program objectives and procedures for measuring their attainment. Moreover, if objectives are stated in easily measurable terms, the whole assessment process will be simplified. Fewer advanced statistical techniques will be needed, and this may help to reduce the psychological distance between the staff and the evaluator.

Readers who are interested in learning more about this point of view might consult Popham (1975, 1981).

Example: The Goal-Oriented Approach

Mark Wilson works in the office of research and evaluation in a large city school district. He is assigned one region of the district and his job is to help schools in this area solve their evaluation problems.

A new principal was recently appointed at Pine Crest School and she sets up a meeting with Mark to talk about the school's evaluation. When he arrives, she shows him the report that had been written the year before and complains that it doesn't help her at all to improve the school's program. "It says that the fourth graders gained 1.2 year's growth in reading on the average last year and only 1.0 year's growth in mathematics, which is fine, as far as it goes, but it doesn't go far enough. It's good to know about overall results, but I also need to know about specific pieces." Then she says, "Here's the reading curriculum," and pushes some papers across the desk toward Mark. "I can't figure out which skills we should work on. Do these kids know how to work with punctuation or don't they? Show me where in this report it tells me that."

Mark skims through the report and sees that the summary statistics that were reported do not provide any specific information about skill areas such as sentence structure or punctuation. He explains that if this is the sort of information she wants, then he will help her develop an evaluation that will answer these questions. "First," he says, "we have to identify some instructional goals in very specific terms, such as 'Students will know how to use the period to mark the ends of sentences and abbreviations.' If we can work together to develop a set of specific instructional objectives, then we can build an evaluation that will provide the kind of information you want."

Over the course of the next three months Mark meets with representatives from each of the grade levels and helps them develop a set of key instructional objectives. Then they meet to establish reasonable performance expectations for their students. In most cases, the teachers feel that the majority of the students, say 70 or 80%, will be able to master these skills by the end of the year. In some cases they know that the skills are more difficult and expect a lower percentage to learn them.

During the next three months the teachers work under Mark's direction to develop some exercises that can be used to test students' performance on these identified objectives. Mark works closely with the teachers to be sure that they develop objectives that can be measured easily and that they write fair and unbiased questions relating to each of the specific topics.

By the end of the year they have developed a series of exercises that are linked directly to the curricular objectives. The exercises are administered to all of the students, the teachers score them, and Mark uses the information to prepare a report for the principal.

The principal is delighted with the information. For example, she learns that 78% of the fourth grade students are able to use periods properly at the ends of sentences and in abbreviations. The rest of the information is equally specific and relates directly to the curriculum objectives that have been established.

The Decision-Focused Approach

The decision-focused approach to evaluation emphasizes the systematic provision of information for program management and operation.

According to this point of view, information is most valuable if it helps program managers make better decisions. Therefore, evaluation activities should be planned to coordinate with the decision needs of program staff. Data collection and reporting are undertaken to promote more effective program management.

Moreover, since programs change as they are implemented and mature, decision makers' needs will change, and the evaluation will have to adapt to these changes. During the planning phase program developers need information about problems and the capacity of the organization to address them. During the implementation phase administrators need information about the processes that are taking place. When the program is mature, the crucial decisions will be made on the basis of outcomes. As a result, the decision-focused evaluator must understand the program development cycle and be prepared to provide different kinds of information at different points in time.

Decision-focused evaluators think in terms of an information system for gathering, analyzing, and reporting information keyed to specific decision points during the life of the program. Ideally the program and the evaluation system are developed together, but this does not always occur. Often the evaluator is consulted after the program has been initiated.

Not only do general information needs change over the life of the program, but at any particular stage there are differences in the kinds of information needed by different individuals. For example, if a school adopted a reading program in which students were placed in homogeneous groups for instruction at the beginning of the year, the teacher would need initial estimates of students' abilities to make those placement decisions. Similarly, if reading grades were to be given at the midpoint of the semester, then more precise information would be needed at this point in time. Meanwhile, the school principal will need different kinds of information about student performance to make administrative decisions.

Typically, the decision-focused evaluator works backward from the various decision points to design information-gathering activities that provide relevant data to reduce uncertainty in decision making. The decision-focused evaluator needs two kinds of information from clients. First, he or she must know the important decision points in each program cycle. Second, he or she needs to know the kinds of information that might illuminate each decision. Of course, some decisions are made on the basis of politics and other considerations that are not information related. The decision-focused evaluator tries to identify those instances in which information will be relevant to a decision and develop a systematic process to provide meaningful data at those points in time.

The strengths of the decision-focused approach are its attention to specific needs of decision makers and the increased impact this may have on program-related decisions. To the extent that specific decision points exist and there is relevant information to be considered, the decision-focused approach can produce highly influential evaluations.

The weaknesses of the approach stem from the fact that many important decisions are not made at a specific point in time, but occur through a gradual process of accretion. Furthermore, many decisions are not "data-based" but rely on subjective impressions, politics, "gut feelings," personnel needs, and so on. In such cases a decision-focused evaluation may even act as a positive influence toward more rational decision making.

Implications for focusing the evaluation. As you might imagine, the process of focusing an evaluation from the decision-oriented perspective begins with the decision makers themselves. In most instances this will be the program director, but it might also include a board of directors, client groups, staff members who have supervisory responsibility, and others. The evaluator needs to determine who are the key decision makers and to consult with them.

Then the evaluator tries to learn as much as possible about the decision context: What kinds of decisions are made? Who makes them? What alternatives exist? What kinds of information might be meaningful? For example, if normative data from a standardized achievement tests are irrelevant to the program staff for the decision at hand, then there is no point in collecting them. As an evaluator, you can provide a variety of different kinds of information; the choice should be based upon the relevance of the data to a particular decision.

In focusing an evaluation the evaluator must develop data-gathering strategies that are meaningful for the specific program decisions and decision makers that exist. To accomplish this the evaluator must become quite familiar with the program and the staff. Thus a decision-focused evaluation is a collaborative relationship that involves detailed information about program components and staff actions.

Decision-focused models of evaluation were proposed by a number of researchers; two of the most thorough ones were described by Stufflebeam et al. (1971) and by Alkin (1969).

Example: The Decision-Focused Approach

The Melrose County Human Relations Cooperative is a community-based organization that provides a wide variety of social services to the residents in the county. The cooperative recently received funding to provide refugee assistance to the growing number of Indo-Chinese immigrants who are settling in the area, and Jason Baxter, the director of the cooperative, wants an evaluator to help monitor the success of their efforts. Though the cooperative had worked with Central American and South American refugees in the past, they have not provided any services for immigrants from Indo-China and other parts of Asia. Consequently, Jason is concerned about the appropriateness of some of the services they might offer. He contacts Yvonne Driscoll, an evaluation consultant who works in the county, to discuss an evaluation of the project.

Yvonne comes to meet with Jason to plan the evaluation, and she asks him to describe the project, the choices he has, and the sort of actions he might take at different points in time. Jason explains that the cooperative's initial plan is to set up classes in English as a second language (ESL), job training programs geared toward two or three local occupations, food preparation classes, and counseling sessions. Each of these activities has worked with other immigrant groups in the past.

Jason admits that they are not sure whether the programs will be effective under the present circumstances. Yvonne probes further to discover what actions might be taken if the program is not having the anticipated results, when these actions might be taken, and what kinds of evidence would provide meaningful indicators of success or failure. Together, they work out a monitoring timetable that correlates decision points and information needs. For example, Jason indicates that he is particularly concerned about the clerical training programs and thinks that he ought to be able to tell within two or three weeks if the curriculum needs major changes. On the other hand, the ESL courses need to continue for four to six months before it will be possible to make useful comparisons between progress and expectations.

In addition, Yvonne designs simple forms for staff members to report on the number of clients who are participating in various programs. She also develops more elaborate systems for collecting information that relates to the more important program events.

Though a number of changes may be necessary during the year, the basic evaluation system that is laid out at this initial meeting will probably continue in use throughout the year. It will help Jason adjust the program to meet the needs of the new immigrant population.

The User-Oriented Approach

During the 1970s evaluation became a standard component of almost all publicly funded social programs. As a result, people who could conduct evaluations were quite busy. However, rather than being wholly pleased with this situation, they began to voice concerns over the impact of their efforts. Some evaluators complained that their reports made little difference in program operations. Data were being reported up the chain of command in compliance with regulations but they did not seem to have any impact at the local level. Whether one did a research-like study or focused on the degree to which the program objectives had been met, the results were not used as much as evaluators thought they should be. A common refrain was that the evaluation reports were just gathering dust on administrators' bookshelves or in agency archives.

In response to these concerns, researchers began to investigate the problem of evaluation utilization. They accumulated empirical evidence about elements that limited or enhanced the use of information. A number of positive factors were identified, including direct involvement of key decision makers, timeliness of the information, and sensitivity to the organizational context. More than anything else, personal involvement seemed to play a key role in promoting evaluation use.

Because many of these positive factors could be influenced by the behavior of the evaluator, a number of researchers developed new approaches that placed greater emphasis on enhancing the use of information. We call these "user-oriented" approaches to evaluation, and, as you might imagine, potential users of information are the focal points.

The user-oriented evaluator is conscious of a number of elements that are likely to affect the utility of the evaluation. These include human elements such as style, rapport, and sensitivity; contextual factors such as pre-existing conditions, organizational features, and community influence; and the manner in which the evaluation is conducted and reported. The single most important element is probably the involvement of potential users throughout the evaluation. For example, a user-oriented evaluator might focus an evaluation by forming a working group of representatives from all key user groups. This user work team would help to frame the evaluation, to identify important questions, to select measurement strategies, to review preliminary results and factor them into actions, and finally to receive the results of the evaluation. The user-oriented evaluator tries to involve key constituents throughout the process of the evaluation, so they are privy to information as it comes to light. There is less emphasis on "the final report" and more on continuing involvement and regular communication.

The user-oriented evaluator places primary emphasis on people and the way they use information. Concerns about research design and data analysis techniques or the clarification of goals and objectives may also be evident, but they receive less emphasis. For example, if the users' needs change during the course of the program, a user-oriented evaluation may change. This is possible in a user-oriented evaluation, though it would be an anathema in a research or goal-oriented study. The user-oriented evaluator accepts the fact that there is a certain amount of unpredictability in any program setting. External events affect programs, and a useful evaluation should be adaptable.

The strengths of the user-oriented approach are its concern with individuals who care about the program and its attention to information that is meaningful to them. This not only makes the evaluation more relevant but creates a sense of ownership that increases the likelihood that the results will be used.

The weaknesses of this approach are its reliance on a stable user group and its susceptibility to greater influence from some interests than others. User groups can change composition frequently and this can disrupt the continuity of activities. Finally, those who are more vocal or more persuasive can have undue influence. Moreover, it is difficult to ensure that all interests are represented.

Implications for focusing the evaluation. If you adopt an approach that emphasizes the use of information by clients, then you must pay greater attention to the people who influence program decisions and the context in which the project operates. Most user-oriented evaluators try to identify people who are likely to be users of evaluation information, enhance their participation in the evaluation process, and increase their feelings of "ownership" of the results of that process. Thus the evaluator who adopts this approach pays more attention to contextual and interpersonal issues than to the tenets of research or the demands of measurement.

User-oriented evaluators are more likely than other evaluators to become closely involved in program activities. They act more as internal agents than external agents. To a certain extent the user-oriented evaluator becomes a student of the organization as well as an observer of program dynamics. The evaluator is less an expert on a set of techniques than a collaborator trying to respond in a meaningful way to organizational realities. The approach is cooperative; the evaluator seeks to gain an understanding of the way the program functions and the needs of the people who influence decisions. Patton (1986) characterizes this as an "active, reactive, adaptive" approach in which the evaluator proposes ideas to the user group, responds to their suggestions, and adapts the evaluation to the needs of the clients.

The evaluator who adopts a user-oriented approach must be an effective communicator. Since interactions with clients and program staff can affect the utilization of the results, communication skills are important. Even written reports are presented in ways that will increase their utility: short, direct summaries rather than lengthy, academic reports; pictorial presentations and graphs rather than lengthy prose passages.

The reader who is interested in learning more about this approach is directed to Patton (1986), Alkin, Daillak, and White (1979), and Braskamp and Brown (1980).

Example: The User-Oriented Approach

The Community Mental Health Agency of Westpark has been operating successfully for five years with little or no direct scrutiny from the city council. Recently, a new city council was elected on a platform of fiscal conservatism, and they have ordered evaluations of all city agencies. To comply with the city council's mandate, the mayor's office contracted with a number of local consultants to conduct evaluations of all agencies.

Henry Braverman and Associates received the contract to evaluate the Mental Health Agency. When Henry took the job, he realized that a lot of people were keenly interested in the project. Obviously, the director of the agency and the staff wanted a favorable report to justify continued funding. Since the mayor's office had to report to the council, they needed sound evidence to support any recommendations they made. The city council wanted to reduce expenditures and were likely to use the evaluations as justifications for their decisions. Even the townspeople had a vested interest in the information, particularly those who were clients of the agency, such as outpatients who received counseling and group therapy services, or women who were the victims of domestic violence and received emergency counseling. All of these people, as well as the community in general, were keenly interested in the information that might be contained in the Braverman report.

Of course, Braverman wants his report to have an impact, and he is confident that his firm is going to be able to produce meaningful information. However, he wants to ensure that it is not going to be buried on a shelf somewhere and ignored in the decisions that are going to be made. As a result, he decides to involve representatives of the key constituent groups throughout the evaluation process.

He begins by forming a steering committee and asks the city council, the mayor's office, the community mental health staff and administration, and key citizen groups to appoint representatives to work with him. He works with the steering committee to frame the questions that will be addressed by the evaluation, and to go over everything that is done while the project is taking place.

With the committee's help, Braverman focuses the evaluation itself on two issues. The first task is to document the level of services that are delivered by the agency. The second is to try to determine the continuing need for services that exists in the community—both those needs that have been met in the past and those that are going unfulfilled.

The first question proves to be the easier of the two to address because there are extensive records available from the mental health agency to document the kinds of contacts it makes and the impact it has on the community. To address the second question Braverman decides to form additional special interest working groups. For example, an adolescent working group is formed to help Braverman gather information about substance abuse among youth. Another special task force is formed to examine the needs of the senior citizens for mental health and counseling services.

As the information is gathered it is shared with the steering committee. In this way all of the interested groups know what is going on throughout the course of the evaluation. In fact, by the time the evaluation reports are due in the mayor's office, the contents of Braverman's report are well known. Both the agency's strengths in working with the elderly, with women, and with outpatient therapy, and its deficiencies in serving the needs of adolescents and alcohol and drug abusers, are well known by the people who are interested in city services. In fact, the director of the agency initiates some changes independent of the funding decisions of the city council.

Ultimately, the community health agency receives one of the smallest budget cuts. The council member who had served on the evaluation steering committee is instrumental in defending the agency before her colleagues on the council. Her clear understanding of the situation is apparent during the debates over the funding decisions.

The Responsive Approach

The responsive approach is for many the most dramatically different of the five perspectives presented here because of its perspective on the purposes of evaluation and the methods to be used to achieve them. Responsive evaluation is guided by the belief that the only meaningful evaluation is one that seeks to understand an issue from the multiple points of view of all people who have a stake in the program. The responsive evaluator does not believe that there is a single answer to a program question that can be found by using tests, questionnaires, or statistical analyses. Instead, each person who is influenced by a program perceives it in a unique manner, and an evaluator can try to help answer program-related questions by portraying reality through the eyes of concerned constituents. The goal of the responsive evaluator is to facilitate efforts to understand the program from multiple perspectives.

The responsive evaluator also adopts a different approach to research and the problem of understanding organizational dynamics. Responsive evaluation is usually characterized by qualitative, naturalistic studies, not quantitative ones. Rather than gathering quantified data through structured tests or questionnaires, the responsive evaluator relies on direct and indirect observation of events and impressionistic interpretation of these data. One observes, records, winnows through data, checks preliminary understandings with program participants, and tries to build models that reflect the insights of various groups. In this way the evaluation attempts to be responsive to the people who have a stake in the results rather than to the demands of a research design or a measurement technique.

Of course, the responsive evaluator does not eschew measurement and analysis altogether. One important element in a responsive evaluation may be the collection and synthesis of data. However, traditional testing and instrumentation are generally of secondary importance. The primary data of responsive evaluation are direct and indirect observations, and the chief form of reporting is the case study or descriptive portrayal.

The evaluator who adopts the responsive point of view acts as an organizational anthropologist, seeking to understand reality from the perspective of program staff, program participants, and other groups who are affected by the program itself.

The strengths of the responsive approach are its sensitivity to multiple points of view and its ability to accommodate ambiguous or poorly focused concerns. Responsive evaluators can operate in situations in which there are differences between the concerns of different groups because they can embody these conflicting points of view in a meaningful way. Similarly, a responsive evaluation can facilitate the problem identification process by providing information that may help people understand issues better.

The weaknesses of the responsive approach are its reluctance to establish priorities or simplify information for decision making, and the fact that it is practically impossible to take into account the perspectives of all concerned groups.

Implications for focusing the evaluation. The responsive evaluator spends a great deal of time talking with clients, observing program activities as they take place, trying to discern underlying purposes and concerns, and conceptualizing problems and issues from various points of view. Consequently, the evaluator must be able to empathize with others. He or she must not jump to conclusions but, rather, verify and recheck hypotheses against primary data sources. This requires patience as well as sensitivity.

Instead of bringing external beliefs to bear, the evaluator tries to draw out issues and problems from staff, participants, clients, and other concerned individuals. Rather than being an external agent, the responsive evaluator acts like a counselor, helping participants clarify their own understanding. Consequently, a person who adopts this approach to evaluation needs to be a good observer. He or she must be able to adapt to differing points of view without imposing external judgments.

The responsive evaluator must be trained in the use of qualitative research techniques. This includes open-ended strategies for data collection, such as observation and semi-structured interviewing. This also includes techniques for organizing and analyzing qualitative data, such as impressionistic analysis and indexing.

The reader who interested in learning more about the responsive approach might want to read Stake (1975) or Lincoln and Guba (1985).

Example: The Responsive Approach

Dr. M.J. Stevens is the Director of Instruction for one of the nation's largest private vocational school chains. The school specializes in training people for careers in computers and computer-related industries, and also provides vocational education in almost all health-related careers, such as nursing, lab technician, and dental assistant.

Dr. Stevens is proud of the success that the schools are having, but is frustrated by a number of nagging personnel problems among the teaching staff. Despite all efforts, turnover remains high. For example, over a two-year period Dr. Stevens was able to increase teachers' salaries by almost 25%, but this did not cure the high turnover rate. No sooner did Dr. Stevens fill a vacancy than a new one occurred.

Frustrated and confused, Dr. Stevens seeks the help of an outside evaluator who has been recommended by a close friend. When Marge Justin receives the phone call from the director of instruction of the private school, she assumes that the school administrators are interested in assessing instructional outcomes. When she meets Dr. Stevens for the first time, she is surprised that the discussion has nothing to do with student outcomes. Instead, Dr. Stevens explains the problem with staff and says, "I'm concerned about staff turnover. I don't really understand what the problems are, and I don't know what to do."

Marge can see immediately that Dr. Stevens cannot explain the nature of the problem, and that this, in fact, is the issue the evaluation needs to address. Therefore, Marge suggests that she can conduct an evaluation to help Dr. Stevens understand the culture of the school and illuminate the causes of the high turnover among staff. "Moreover," she explains, "since the turnover issue affects students as well as the administration, they should be included in the study. If you really want to understand what is going on, then everybody who has a stake in this issue should be consulted."

Marge spends the next two months in and around the schools. She observes classes, and she visits the library and study areas to see how students and staff conduct themselves. She speaks with students, with teachers, and even talks with a couple of employers who have employed graduates from the school in the past. She lets the ideas and perceptions of the people she talks with suggest where to go next and what to discuss.

This process illuminates a number of concerns. For example, the teachers feel that their jobs have very little status. The problem is not one of salary, it involves the perceptions of their fellow teachers in other institutions. Teachers at the vocational school feel that they are at the bottom of the totem pole and they are just waiting for an opportunity to move up to a "real school." Yet they are not totally dissatisfied. Teachers explain that the actual classroom interactions are extremely gratifying. The students are motivated and appreciate the teachers' efforts. One of the teachers says, "You know, I resent being paid by the hour. If they would pay me a salary, I would feel much better about teaching even though the amount of money is exactly the same." Students are resentful at the high turnover among teachers. They bad-mouth the school among themselves and occasionally to employers in the community.

From all of these conversations and observations, the evaluator is able to put together a description of the school for Dr. Stevens that provides new ways of looking at teacher turnover. Her report provides ideas that can be used to address the problem and raises questions that have not been previously considered.

Over the next year, Dr. Stevens does, in fact, change the way teachers are paid. In addition, a "career ladder" is put into effect, and teachers are given new titles to provide a greater sense of continuity and progression for the staff.

Comparing Approaches to Evaluation

In the previous section we described five different approaches to program evaluation. Table 1 summarizes some of the key elements of each approach. While they differ in many obvious ways, they also have important underlying similarities.

Similarities. All five approaches to evaluation share one fundamental goal: to provide information that will help people assess and/or enhance

TABLE 1
Five Approaches to Evaluation

Approach	Emphasis	Focusing Issues	Evaluator's Role
Experimental	Research design	What effects result from program activities and can they be generalized?	Expert/scientist
Goal-oriented	Goals and objectives	What are the program's goals and objectives and how can they be measured?	Measurement specialist
Decision-focused	Decision making	Which decisions need to be made and what information will be relevant?	Decision support person
User-oriented	Information users	Who are the intended information users and what information will be most useful?	Collaborator
Responsive	Personal understanding	Which people have a stake in the program and what are their points of view?	Counselor/facilitator

program operations. In each case the stock in trade of the evaluator—be it an experimental evaluation or a responsive evaluation—is information. That information may be a generalizable statement about the comparative impact of alternative treatment conditions, or it may be a descriptive portrayal of different points of view that highlights inconsistencies and incongruities in program operations. It may be a measure of the degree of the completion of various behavioral objectives or an interim report for board members who are about to decide on future program funding. In every case the evaluator is an information provider, and the worth of the evaluation is tied to the value of the information that is provided.

Another element that is common to all these approaches is their concern for accuracy. Although the manner in which they define accuracy differs, each of the five types of evaluators strives to provide valid information. The experimental evaluator embodies this concern in the way he or she structures the evaluation task. The goal-oriented evaluator stresses the clear statement and measurement of objectives. The decision-focused evaluator and the user-oriented evaluator recognize that they may mislead clients into making erroneous decisions if they provide sloppy or inappropriate information. The responsive evaluator recognizes that different people see the world in different ways and tries to provide information that is meaningful from multiple perspectives. Accuracy is the common thread that underlies all of these approaches.

Differences. There are also distinct differences between the five approaches. One way in which they differ is the research technique they use. Some employ quantitative strategies which stress simplification and control while others incorporate qualitative approaches that emphasize diversity and multiple points of view.

Clearly, the experimental and goal-oriented approaches to evaluation use primarily quantitative techniques while the responsive approach employs mostly qualitative ones. The other approaches use techniques from both traditions. For example, the decision-focused evaluator may relax some of the demands of research design to meet the needs of the local decision context. The user-oriented evaluator often uses naturalistic strategies to be sensitive to individual points of view.

Another way in which the five evaluation approaches differ is the criteria that are used as the basis for action and judgment. Some approaches invoke external, prespecified criteria; others rely more on internal standards. For example, the evaluator who adopts the experimental approach brings a set of external criteria to bear during the design of the study to ensure the validity of conclusions. The goal-oriented evaluator has a preconceived strategy for specifying program goals and objectives and quantifying their measurement, though this strategy encourages the specification of locally relevant goals. In contrast, the user-focused evaluator often adopts the same criteria of importance, success, and meaningfulness as do the users. At the extreme, the responsive evaluator believes that only personal perceptions and measures are meaningful to involved individuals.

Finally, the five approaches can be compared on the basis of scientific objectivity. Experimental studies are highly scientific, utilizing random assignment, control groups, and other design strategies to ensure that conclusions are not biased by human judgment. Similarly, the evaluator who focuses on the attainment of program goals works to construct objective measures of relevant variables. Decision-focused and user-oriented evaluations can include more subjective elements, if these are relevant to decision makers or other users. A responsive evaluation can be highly subjective and may even present unresolved and conflicting points of view.

Summary. We have outlined five different approaches to evaluation. It is up to the evaluator to select the technique or combination of techniques that are appropriate in a given situation. The effective evaluator brings together a collection of methods and approaches to fit the needs of each client and may play many different roles—expert, collaborator, decision support person, or facilitator—in different situations.

Clarifying Your Own Approach to Evaluation

Each of us has unique beliefs and attitudes about evaluation based on our own training and experience. If you have not recently done so, it would be worthwhile to review your own approach to evaluation. The following questions may help.

(1) How do you define the term "evaluation?"
(2) What do you think the goal of evaluation should be?
(3) What techniques would you employ in conducting an evaluation?
(4) What do you think the client's responsibilities should be?
(5) How would you compare your approach to evaluation to the five models we have presented here?

Chapter 3
How to Gather Information

If all social programs were fundamentally alike, or if one approach to evaluation were equally appropriate in all situations, it would not be necessary to gather a great deal of information about a program before setting out to evaluate it. Fortunately, this is not the case. Programs are diverse, and evaluators can select from a rich conceptual menu. To take advantage of this diversity, evaluators must take sufficient time to familiarize themselves with each program they set out to evaluate so they can tailor their evaluation to fit.

The failure of an evaluator to inform him- or herself systematically about several aspects of a program before setting out to evaluate it can result in costly mistakes and seriously undermine the usefulness of the eventual product. Consider these examples:

- An evaluator used an experimental approach to evaluate the effectiveness of three alcohol dependency treatment approaches, but did not learn that one program was plagued by extreme staff turnover and a dictatorial director. By focusing exclusively on outcomes, he produced a misleading report rather than a useful one.
- An evaluator using a goal-oriented approach spent months developing tests to match the objectives of a reading curriculum. After he produced the set of completed instruments, he learned that the special reading class met for only 30 minutes a day, too short a period of time to administer his tests.
- An evaluator hired by the State Highway Patrol to study the effects of a new highway safety program reported in May that the program was highly effective. Unfortunately, the Joint Appropriations Committee of the State Legislature had voted to discontinue funds for the program in April because there was "no evidence of impact."

Such errors can be attributed to a lack of information about the program and clients needs' for evaluation at the time the evaluation was designed. They could have been avoided had the evaluator followed a comprehensive plan for gathering appropriate information at the outset. As an evaluator you need to know as much as you can about the program—the purposes of the evaluation, the audiences for it, and the limitations imposed by time, money, and the availability of information—before you arrive at a plan for the evaluation and begin to undertake it. Typically, you do not have much time to gather this information, and at this stage you are not being paid to do it. So, you need to plan in advance what information is most important to know, and obtain it as efficiently as possible.

Most of the information needed initially can be organized into three broad questions:

- What is the program?
- Why is it being evaluated?
- What constraints limit the evaluation?

Each of these questions is only a starting place. Each suggests a series of more specific questions, which we will discuss next. The evaluator will require additional detail in specific areas depending on the immediate situation and the views of evaluation held by the client and the evaluator. For example, the goal-oriented evaluator will spend additional time determining the objectives of the program, while the decision-based evaluator will need to know a great deal about the development cycle of the program and the types of decisions to be made in coming months. We will consider these special information needs later. The evaluator will interview key program personnel to get answers to these questions. Most will come from the project director.

What Is the Program?

Acquiring rudimentary familiarity with the program is the first order of business. The evaluator should spend at least an hour listening to the person most familiar with the overall operation of the program "tell about it." From the outset the evaluator needs an organizing framework to help remember the wealth of detail that is likely to emerge. In the most fundamental terms, the evaluator needs to know (1) what the program is intended to do, (2) who is supposed to benefit from it, (3) who operates the program, and (4) what it is that they do. Often these are the first topics a client will mention when asked to tell about the program.

However, at times the administrator of a program will assume that all such programs follow a similar pattern that is familiar to the evaluator.

For example, the administrator of a program to prevent substance abuse may describe her program as a "social inoculation approach emphasizing refusal skills" and assume that this description means the same thing to the evaluator that it does to her. When this situation occurs the evaluator can guide the interview to touch upon the following:

Clients
- Who is served by the program?
- How do they come to participate?
- Do they differ in systematic ways from non-participants?

Goals
- What is the program intended to do for the people it serves?
- Have formal goals and objectives been identified? What are they?
- Which goals or objectives are most important? Is more time spent trying to accomplish certain objectives than others?
- How do staff members judge how well they are doing at accomplishing their goals?
- If the program were successful, what would you expect to see happening?

Process
- What is the general approach of the program?
- What types of activities are there?
- What is the schedule of activities?

Organization
- Where are the services provided? Are there important differences among the sites?
- Who provides the services? How large is the staff?
- How is the program funded?
- How is the program administered? What is the organization hierarchy?

Example: The Midfield Preschool Program

The director of the Midfield Preschool, Ms. Timms, contacted Dr. Smith about conducting an evaluation of the preschool program. In her initial telephone conversation with Dr. Smith, Ms. Timms told him that she directed a preschool program for a local school district. She wanted an evaluation report to share with parents and the local school board, but did not know how to go about doing an evaluation herself. Dr. Smith said he might be able to help, and scheduled a meeting to discuss the evaluation.

Dr. Smith began the meeting by asking Ms. Timms to describe the preschool program. She told him first that it was a half-day modified Montessori approach aimed at "at-risk" children. Dr. Smith then helped Ms. Timms to expand her description, first asking more specific questions about the children who participated. She explained that the program was limited to children who had completed their fourth birthdays by September 12 and who had a "developmental lag."

"We send out announcements to parents informing them that the district has a preschool program for children who might need special help to prepare them for kindergarten," she said. She went on to explain that parents who are interested bring their child for a developmental assessment in May. Children who score lowest on a developmental screening test but who have achieved a sufficient level of social independence are admitted to the program in order of their score, until 64 positions have been filled.

Dr. Smith asked how participation in the preschool program was intended to benefit the children. Ms. Timms explained that the overall goal of the program was to give children an "added boost" so they would be able to succeed in school in the years to come. She pointed out the program's brochure, which stated, "The Midfield Preschool Program provides stimulation to accelerate students' social, physical, and cognitive development." Then she clarified, "All three are important, but we stress social and cognitive development more than physical for most of the children." When Dr. Smith asked how teachers kept track of children's progress in those areas, Ms. Timms produced a list of skills which teachers checked off for each child as they were acquired.

Subsequently, Dr. Smith asked about the organization of the preschool program. He started by asking Ms. Timms whether all 64 children came to the same place. "Oh, we never work with more than 8 children at a time," Ms. Timms began. She explained that the program operates four preschools, located in small houses owned by the school district in different areas of the city. There is one teacher and one aide at each school. Children come for half a day, with one group of 8 in the morning and another group of 8 in the afternoon.

When Dr. Smith asked whether there were any important differences among the four schools, Ms. Timms smiled. "Well, the Blake Street Cottage is definitely unique," she said. "Ms. Applebee is the teacher there, and she tends to do things her own way. She's an excellent teacher, but I have a hard time getting her to use the district program. She has her own ideas and insists on using her own materials."

Dr. Smith asked what the district program was. Ms. Timms explained that each session was divided into four parts. The first 25 minutes were devoted to structured group activities emphasizing language. Children listened to a brief story or nursery rhyme, and talked about it, acted out parts, or learned a song about it. Sometimes there was show and tell. Next, there was an hour of Montessori play involving the guided use of Montessori equipment. This was followed by a snack. Finally, there was a 35-minute activity period which was devoted to instruction in cognitive skills. Children learned to count beads and string them by color, to identify shapes and place them in holes, to order things from largest to smallest, and so on. "Except at Blake Street," added Ms. Timms. "You'd need to visit there to know what they do."

With this much information, Dr. Smith felt he knew enough about the Midfield Preschool Program to be able to imagine a way to evaluate it.

However, he still needed to know more about the purposes an evaluation might serve, and what constraints of time, money, and availability of information would limit his potential activities.

Why Is the Evaluation Being Conducted?

Once the evaluator understands in broad terms what the program is about, the next step in focusing the evaluation is to arrive at an understanding of why the evaluation is being conducted and what purposes it should serve. This process involves the exchange of views between the client and the evaluator, an exchange in which the evaluator often takes the lead because of his or her expertise in this area.

In Chapter 2, we identified several purposes that an evaluation may be intended to serve. It may be undertaken to satisfy a routine accountability requirement, to assist program managers and staff by providing them with more objective and complete information than they already have, or to provide information for advisory groups, program clients, governing boards, or funding agents. We also pointed out that clients vary in the interests which motivate them to seek an evaluator and in the expectations that they have for evaluation. The flexible, creative evaluator considers the purposes, interests, and expectations of the client as well his or her own preferences in formulating an evaluation plan. The match between the evaluator's approach and the needs and expectations of the client is discussed more fully in Chapter 4.

It is not sufficient merely to ask the client why he or she wants an evaluation conducted and what purposes it might serve. Program managers frequently find themselves in the position of requesting assistance in program evaluation without having a clear idea of what evaluation entails or what value it can be to them. The impetus for a program evaluation is often an evaluation requirement established by the funding agent. In these instances, the program manager may not realize that the evaluation can provide him or her with useful information or address more than one audience. Here the evaluator can provide a valuable service by expanding the client's view of evaluation, while seeing that the accountability purpose of the funding agent is also met.

The evaluator should also bear in mind that an evaluation usually has several potential audiences. Clients, staff, management, funding boards or agencies, and the general public all have a direct interest in most social programs. These groups typically have different needs for information and view the purposes of an evaluation differently. For example, staff who feel that they have done the best they could with minimal resources may hope that the evaluation will point out the need for additional funding for such things as new equipment. Funding agents may want to know how much they have gotten for their money in quantity and quality of services and results. It is possible to provide useful information to several audiences in a single evaluation.

Of course, the program director or governing board who contracts for an evaluation may not be interested in having others participate in focusing it and may want to control access to the evaluation once it is completed. Consequently, the evaluator must frame his or her role carefully, respecting the interest of the primary client while recognizing that there may be other interested parties who have a stake in the program and the evaluation. In some situations, it may be appropriate to involve these groups in focusing the evaluation; in others, it may not.

In a meeting with the client the evaluator can best determine the potential purposes for the evaluation, the client's interests, the client's expectations, and the possibility of addressing multiple audiences by asking direct and indirect questions and by offering suggestions. The following types of questions can be asked:

Immediate purposes
- Why is the program to be evaluated?
- How could the evaluation be most valuable to you?

Expectations
- How would you describe previous evaluations of the program?
- How could previous evaluations have been made more valuable?
- What kind of information do you think the evaluation should contain?

Concerns and interests
- Do you have any concerns about the program at this time?
- Have any major changes in the program occurred recently?
- Are any major changes anticipated in the near future?
- What information about the program would be most useful to you? to your staff? to your clients? to your supervisors or funding agency?

Other audiences for the evaluation
- What groups of people are involved with the program or are affected by it?
- What sort of information about the program would be most valuable to each of these groups?
- Should representatives from other groups be interviewed while planning the evaluation?

- Which groups should receive information about the evaluation when it is completed? Should special reports be directed at specific groups?

Example: The Midfield Preschool Program

When Ms. Timms first contacted Dr. Smith regarding an evaluation of the Midfield Preschool Program, she mentioned that she "wanted an evaluation report to share with parents and the local school board." Later, when Dr. Smith asked her specifically why she wanted an evaluation of the program, she provided additional information. "The program is federally funded, and we have to submit an evaluation annually," she explained. "But in the past, the annual evaluations have never been of any value to us. We simply report the average number of skills from our checklist that children acquired during the year. It satisfied the requirement, but it wasn't helpful to anyone, really. I want something that would really indicate to parents and to the school board that the program is effective and deserves support."

Dr. Smith asked Ms. Timms if she had any ideas about the sort of information she would like to be able to report. She had thought of several possibilities. "I've always thought it would be good to do a long-term study of our children," she suggested. "We don't really know what happens to them after they leave our program." She also mentioned that she would like to know how the children compared at the end of the program to others their age. "I feel certain we are having a large impact on them," she said, "but I don't know how to document it."

Dr. Smith asked whether Ms. Timms had any concerns with the program. She said there were no major concerns or issues. "All my teachers are very good," she said, "and they have excellent rapport with the children and their parents. There is one thing, though. It appears to me that the parents don't really understand what we are trying to do. I have the impression that they think we're supposed to take all the responsibility and they do not need to do anything at home to follow-up."

Dr. Smith suggested that information about the parent follow-up also might be useful to teachers, and added that one purpose of the evaluation might be to provide information to teachers that could help them be more effective. Ms. Timms had not been thinking along such lines. It occurred to her that the evaluation might be valuable to teachers if it looked at very specific aspects of the instructional program: the daily use of time, the effectiveness of specific activities, or improved monitoring of children's acquisition of new skills. "I imagine it would be expensive to look at details like that," she said, "but it would be valuable for the staff. I would be happy to have you speak with one of the teachers and one of the aides about it, but I wouldn't want those topics to take the place of learning about our overall effectiveness."

Finally, Dr. Smith asked about significant changes in the program which had recently occurred or were planned for the near future. "This is our third year," Ms. Timms explained. "Three of my teachers have been with the program since it opened, and helped design it. Last year we expanded to include the Blake Street site, and Ms. Applebee transferred from a kindergarten position. I think we're set for next year with no major changes. After that, though, I'm worried that our federal funding is going to decrease and we may have to close one of the sites. My hope is that the district will pick up the difference."

Later that afternoon, Dr. Smith spoke with one of the teachers and one of the parents. The teacher, Ms. Applebee, hoped the evaluation would look at parent involvement and at the effectiveness of the Montessori component. "We could do far more for these children if their parents reinforced our efforts at home," she said. "And I am convinced that the hour we spend on Montessori activities is a big waste of time. I don't think the children use the equipment correctly, and I'm not convinced they learn much from it when they do. I don't use it at all."

The parent, Ms. Lo, spoke positively about the program, but didn't know much about what was actually done in class. When Dr. Smith asked her if she felt well informed about what her child did at the school she said, "Not really. They send home messages, but I can't read them in English. They asked me to visit, but I work in the morning. They should have a meeting at night, or come here in the afternoon."

What Constraints Limit the Evaluation?

The evaluator needs to determine what cannot be done as well as to imagine what can. The scope of the evaluation will be limited by a number of practical considerations; chief among these is money. The contracting client may have a fixed amount budgeted for the evaluation, or may ask the evaluator to propose an amount. In either instance, the size of the program and its operating budget will impose limits. The amount budgeted for evaluation often ranges between 5% and 10% of the operating budget for a special program.

Money usually translates into time in an evaluation, but time considerations may impose independent limits of their own. Frequently, the program's funding cycle dictates a schedule for the evaluation and a deadline for its completion. For some programs, such as those occurring in schools, the program itself has a cycle requiring that certain evaluation activities be conducted during a prescribed period of time. If the evaluation is designed to provide information for specific decisions, it must be completed early enough in the decision process to be of use.

Access to information may pose another constraint. For example, a survey of former participants in a program may provide valuable information. However, it may be impractical to undertake this task depending on the mobility of the former participants and the existence of an up-to-date address file. Data stored in a computer are likely to be more accessible than data stored in paper files. Access to information may also be constrained by concerns with confidentiality or political factors. It is useful to identify these constraints early in the process of gathering information to focus the evaluation.

Finally, the evaluator should consider whether the client might contribute useful resources or services to complement the evaluator's own activities. Frequently clients can assume responsibility for certain kinds of data collection, record keeping, or data retrieval. Where such activity can be done reliably by the client it lessens the work required of the evaluator and frees him or her for other things. Even when the evaluator wishes to conduct his or her own data-gathering or retrieval activities, the willingness of affected program staff and participants to comply with his or her requests should be confirmed. Such cooperation can be thought of as a contributed resource in and of itself.

The following questions will help establish the limitations on the evaluation.

Budget
- Approximately how much money is the client prepared to spend on the evaluation?

Schedule
- By what date is the evaluation report needed?
- Are there interim reporting dates, or should all the information be released at once?

Availability of information
- What information is already available concerning the program?
- How will existing information be accessed (e.g., via computer, paper files in several sites, paper files in one central location?
- What policies exist regarding confidentiality and access to individuals, records, and sites?
- Will key groups or individuals be available to provide information at only certain times?

Additional resources
- Can the organization contribute in-kind resources to the evaluation (e.g., clerical assistance, computer facilities, assistance with data collection)?
- Can staff be relied on to cooperate in data collection or retrieval activities?

Example: The Midfield Preschool Program

Ms. Timms seemed slightly embarrassed when Dr. Smith asked her how much she intended to spend for the evaluation. "I planned to spend from

$3,000 to $5,000," she said. "Do you think that is enough?" Dr. Smith explained that the primary cost of performing the evaluation would be his time. He certainly could address some issues for $3,000 to $5,000, though with a larger budget he would be able to address additional questions. He would have to think about a plan a bit more before being able to tell her how much might be done for this amount.

Ms. Timms explained the timeline she had in mind for the evaluation. It was April now, and school would be out in less than two months. "We send in our required evaluation report in June," she said, "so this year is out. We will have until the end of May next year to complete that. However, the board of education makes its budget decisions in April. It would be good to have something to present them by next March. If we want to present anything to teachers," she continued, "it might be best to bring information to them early in the fall. The spring would be a good time to present information to parents."

The discussion turned to the types of information currently available. Ms. Timms described the folders kept on each child, which included name, date of birth, sex, ethnicity, scores on the developmental test and a test of oral English proficiency, the skills checklist, and teacher comments and reports to parents. She had kept the folders for each child who had ever participated in the project. "That's about all we have," she said. "When they go on to kindergarten and first grade the district has standardized test scores on them, but we've never looked at those. We also have developmental test scores on the students who don't end up in the program. Some of them test too high, and we can't accept them. Some would be eligible, but their parents don't send them when they learn it's a half-day program because they need full-day care."

In addition, Ms. Timms offered her own time and clerical support for the evaluation. "My secretary will have time to do all the typing, and can set up visits, get information out of files, and that sort of thing," she said. "I think the teachers will be very cooperative too," she added. "They want to help in any way they can. If you need to observe in classrooms, I'm sure that will be all right."

Tailoring Additional Information-Gathering
to the Evaluation Approach

In Chapter 2 we described five major approaches to evaluation. Each approach varies in the type of information that it emphasizes. Depending on the evaluation approach that is adopted, additional information may be needed in special areas. The types of additional information required by each approach are summarized in Table 2.

The Experimental Approach

The experimental approach to evaluation usually involves controlled comparisons between the program and other "treatments" and may compare the effectiveness of the program for different types of clients. An evaluator employing this approach may require further information regarding *outcome measures,* including unintended impact of the program.

In situations when the evaluator cannot employ random assignment to control for group differences, he or she will also need extensive information concerning the characteristics of program participants which may be related to the impact of the program. The evaluator may need to consult with the director of the program and experts in the field to understand what these relevant characteristics are. A detailed understanding of the process by which participants are selected for the program provides some insight into their significant characteristics, but other important factors may have nothing to do with the selection process. For example, an alcohol treatment program may be more effective with women than with men, or work better with nonsmokers than with smokers. Unless the evaluator chooses to collect information of clients' smoking habits and gender, these findings will not be known. Comparisons with other treatment programs will be less valid if the smoking habits and gender of the respective clients are unknown as well.

The experimental evaluator will want to know more about *variations in treatment.* If more than one approach to serving clients is used, different approaches can be compared to each other as well as to the control group to determine which is most effective. The evaluator must ask whether the same approach was used in each site or by each staff member and identify systematic differences. He or she may also be interested in learning whether the approach has changed over the years the program has been in operation.

Another concern of the experimental evaluator has to do with *outside influences* on program clients which may affect the impact of the program. An alcoholic seeking to control his or her dependence on alcohol may seek assistance in many places: from Alcoholics Anonymous, from the pastor of his or her church, from a counseling program at work, from family and friends. Each of these influences plays a part in the treatment program. Conversely, a program to reduce smoking located in an organization in which nearly everyone smokes may be far less effective than a similar program in an organization in which

TABLE 2
Additional Information Needs

Evaluation Approach	Special Information Needs
Experimental	Outcome measures
	Client characteristics
	Variation in treatments
	Other influences on clients
	Availability of control groups
Goal-oriented	Specific program objectives
	Criterion-referenced outcome measures
Decision-focused	Stage of program development
	Cycle of decision making
	Data gathering and reporting routines
User-oriented	Personal and organizational dynamics
	Group information needs
	Program history
	Intended uses of information
Responsive	Variation in individual and group perspectives
	Stakeholder concerns
	Program history
	Variation in occasions and sites

smoking is unusual. The evaluator must seek information about such outside influences and consider them in the evaluation.

The Goal-Oriented Approach

The goal-oriented evaluator does not seek to establish the impact of the program by means of a comparison group. Instead, the program's success is measured in terms of the goals it has set for itself. The question this evaluator poses is, Has the program achieved its stated objectives? The evaluator using this approach will seek detailed information concerning the *objectives of the program* and the means to measure their attainment. Frequently, such objectives have not been identified, and a major role of the evaluator may be to assist the program staff in developing them.

When objectives have been identified, the evaluator must determine how to measure their attainment. What measures of performance are currently used? Are adequate measures available, or must they be developed as part of the evaluation? When measures are available, what level of performance is judged to be adequate, and for what proportion of clients? It is important that the evaluator plans to involve program staff in the determination of performance criteria. If new measures are to be used, it is advisable to examine empirical data before setting performance criteria.

The Decision-Focused Approach

The evaluator who selects a decision-focused approach asks the client to anticipate important decisions that the client and other decision makers may face in the future regarding the program, and tries to provide pertinent information to help make those decisions. The evaluator employing this approach conceives of a regular cycle of program decisions, including needs assessment, planning, implementation, and outcomes. To focus this type of evaluation, the evaluator needs to determine the *current stage of program development*. He or she will ask about the history of the program to determine what sort of decisions have already been made, and what sort are likely to follow. The timing of future decisions and the client's specific needs for information to assist in making them will be particularly important.

In addition, the decision-oriented evaluator will want to inquire about existing *procedures for gathering information* to serve the administrative cycle of the program. Needs assessment for program planning and goal setting decisions, monitoring of program implementation for quality control, and the assessment of outcomes for account-ability are all evaluation activities which should be carried out in an ongoing cycle. To the extent they are absent, the evaluator may include consultation in developing such procedures as part of the evaluation contract.

The User-Oriented Approach

The user-oriented evaluator believes that making information available to management to assist in decision making is not enough. This evaluator has observed that decision makers are more likely to benefit from information and make use of it if they have been actively involved in recognizing the need for information and in deciding what informa-tion to collect and how to collect it. He or she is also aware that program decisions are made in social and political contexts and at various levels in the organization. This approach seeks to identify individuals, often representatives of groups, who are potentially able to use the information gathered in an evaluation and to involve them from the start in framing and carrying out the evaluation.

Before the evaluation can be focused the user-oriented evaluator must gather additional information about the *organizational and personal dynamics* of the program setting. Who are the advocates for the program? Which programs compete with it for funding? What individuals or groups oppose the program or have been critical of it in the past? What channels of communication link the program with other parts of a parent organization and with outside organizations? What personal animosities disrupt communication? To understand the current state of these relationships, it is helpful for the evaluator to understand something of their *history* as well. How did the program come about? Did its inception drive funds away from another program or agency? Has the program grown or diminished in size and influence?

The user-oriented evaluator spends additional time to determine the *information needs* of the various groups and key individuals who are affected by the program and have a voice in its future. This evaluator may arrive at a sampling plan to ensure that he or she is able to speak with representatives of each of these groups before a plan for the evaluation is finalized. Short interviews with representative members of constituent groups touching on the issues they believe an evaluation might examine and how they believe the program is doing will provide a much clearer picture of the organizational dynamics and help the evaluator to judge what forum for user involvement will be most productive. If the program is not highly politicized, and the potential exists for constituents to arrive at shared understandings regarding the evaluation, the evaluator may recommend the formation of a user advisory group to guide the evaluation. In a more highly charged situation, the evaluator may propose to consult individually with user groups to keep them involved in the evaluation without bringing them together.

The Responsive Approach

The evaluator who adopts a responsive approach tries to understand the program from the various points of view of its constituents, and proceeds to inform each group by expanding its view of the program. This approach assumes that each of the groups associated with a program understands and experiences it differently and has a valid perspective. The evaluator does not attempt to define the scope of the evaluation narrowly before collecting data; instead, he or she responds to issues and concerns as they arise and are identified by clients.

In order to provide the rich program description which is the particular strength of the responsive approach, the evaluator must determine how best to allocate his or her time among various time-intensive activities, such as observing and interviewing. The evaluator may want to develop a sampling plan for selecting occasions, sites, and individuals. To do this, he or she needs to know how the program varies from occasion to occasion. Do activities vary from day to day? Are there monthly or annual cycles which affect program activities? The evaluator will ask similar questions regarding program sites.

Variation among individuals and groups is at the heart of the evaluator's concern, and additional time will be devoted to determining what groups of individuals are affected by the program and to what extent perspectives within the groups are shared. The responsive evaluator will set out quickly to begin to identify *stakeholder concerns.* This orientation does not focus on decision makers, but identifies all those with a stake in the program. Where other evaluation approaches would be unlikely to attend to the perceptions of the children themselves in an educational program, for example, the responsive evaluator might very well look for ways to describe the program from the children's perspective. He or she will want to ask about the organizational setting as part of the focusing process in order to understand who has an interest in the program. Later, this familiarity with the organizational setting will help the evaluator to interpret differences in viewpoints expressed by various clients and stakeholders.

Like the user-oriented evaluator, the responsive evaluator will ask questions concerning the origins and subsequent *history of the program* because it will help him to understand how the program has arrived at its present form and how particular groups and individuals have come to view it differently. For the user-oriented evaluator, this information is valuable because it helps in conducting a useful evaluation. For the evaluator employing a responsive approach, this information may become a product of the evaluation itself.

Summary

A common weakness in many evaluation studies is that they are focused too soon with too little information. This may occur because the

TABLE 3
A Menu of Questions to Guide Information Gathering

PROGRAM

Clients
- Who is served by the program?
- How do they come to participate?
- Do they differ in systematic ways from nonparticipants?
- What characteristics of clients are likely to be associated with program impact? (experimental)
- What group outside the program or in a different program can be used for comparison? (experimental)

Goals
- What is the program intended to accomplish?
- How do staff determine how well they have attained their goals?
- What formal goals and objectives have been identified?
- Which goals or objectives are most important?
- Is more time spent trying to accomplish certain objectives than others?
- How were objectives arrived at? (goal-oriented)
- What measures of performance are currently used?
- Are current measures adequately matched to program objectives? (goal-oriented, experimental)
- Are adequate measures available elsewhere, or must they be developed as part of the evaluation? (goal-oriented, experimental)
- What level of performance is judged to be adequate, and for what portion of clients? (goal-oriented)
- What unintended impacts might the program have? (experimental)

Organization
- Where are the services provided?
- Are there important differences among the sites?
- Who provides the services?
- How large is the staff?
- How is the program funded?
- How is the program administered?
- What is the organizational hierarchy?

- Who are the advocates for the program? (user-oriented, responsive)
- Which programs compete with it for funding? (user-oriented, responsive)
- What individuals or groups oppose the program or have been critical of it in the past? (user-oriented, responsive)
- What channels of communication link the program with other parts of a parent organization and with outside organizations? (user-oriented)
- What personal animosities disrupt communication? (user-oriented, responsive)

History
- How long has the program been implemented?
- How did the program come about? (user-oriented, responsive)
- Did its inception drive funds away from another program or agency? (user-oriented, responsive)
- Has the program grown or diminished in size and influence? (user-oriented, responsive)
- Have any significant changes occurred in the program recently? (user-oriented)

Process
- What is the general approach of the program?
- What types of activities are there?
- What is the schedule of activities?
- Do activities vary from day to day? (responsive)
- Are there monthly or annual cycles which affect program activities? (responsive)
- How do activities vary from site to site? (responsive, experimental)

PURPOSES

General
- Why is the program to be evaluated?
- How could the evaluation be most valuable to the primary client?
- How would you describe previous evaluations of the program?

(continued)

Table 3 (continued)

Expectations	• How could previous evaluations have been made more valuable?
	• What kind of information does the primary client think the evaluation should contain?
	• What groups of people are involved with the program or are affected by it?
Audiences	• What sort of information about the program would be most valuable to each group associated with the program? (user-oriented)
	• Which groups should receive information about the evaluation when it is completed?
	• Should special reports be directed at specific groups? (user-oriented)
	• Can representatives of interested groups be interviewed in the course of focusing the evaluation? (responsive, user-oriented)
Concerns	• What concerns does the primary client have about the program?
	• What concerns do other groups have regarding the program? (responsive, user-oriented)
	• Are any major changes anticipated in the near future?
	• Are concerns at the current stage focused on needs assessment, design options, processes of implementation, or the effectiveness of outcomes? (decision-focused)
	• What kinds of decisions regarding the program are likely to be made in the near future? (decision-focused, user-oriented)

(continued)

evaluation merely follows a routine pattern established in previous years, or because the evaluator assumes that he or she understands the purposes of an evaluation and the key features of the program it involves without discovering whether these assumptions are correct. The result is likely to be an evaluation which is of little value because it fails to focus on the questions of greatest interest or because it lacks validity. To protect against focusing an evaluation prematurely, we have recom-

Table 3 (continued)

CONSTRAINTS

Budget	• Approximately how much money is the client prepared to spend on the evaluation?
Schedule	• By what date is the evaluation report needed?
	• Are there interim reporting dates, or should all the information be released at once?
	• What cycle or schedule of decision making underlies the need for information? (decision-focused)
Availability	• What information is already available concerning the program?
	• How will existing information be accessed (e.g., via computer, paper files in several sites, paper files in one central location)?
	• What policies exist regarding confidentiality and access to individuals, records, and sites?
	• Will key groups or individuals be available to provide information at only certain times? (User-oriented, responsive)
	• What data gathering routines and procedures are employed? (decision-focused)
Additional	• Can the organization contribute in-kind resources to the evaluation (e.g., clerical assistance, computer facilities, assistance with data collection)?

mended that the evaluator always seek answers to questions in three broad areas before developing an evaluation proposal, regardless of the evaluation approach he intends to employ. The choice of an overall evaluation approach will dictate additional questions as well.

Table 3 is a comprehensive list of questions to assist the evaluator in gathering information before focusing an evaluation. It is not so much an interview guide as it is a menu to remind the evaluator of categories of information and specific areas easily forgotten or overlooked in the press of an interview. Basic topics are listed first, followed by questions pertaining to particular research approaches.

Chapter 4
How to Formulate an Evaluation Plan

The purpose of this chapter is to explain how to use the information you obtain from the questions described in Chapter 3 to formulate a plan for an evaluation. There was a number of reasons why this is a complex subject. For one thing, you do not actually gather all the information before you begin to organize it and synthesize a plan of operation. Instead, all three processes take place simultaneously and interact with one another. As you learn things, you try to organize your knowledge in a way that highlights the evaluation-relevant details and makes planning easier. You also build (and rebuild) tentative plans of action whenever a cluster of features suggests a strategy. As your knowledge base grows these tentative plans may be revised.

It is difficult to describe the interactive planning process because most of it takes place in the mind of the evaluator, leaving no written record to be shared or investigated. Because of this some people might argue that the process is as much art as science. In contrast, we believe that most of what occurs in evaluation planning can be analyzed and described, but we freely admit that some nonanalytic elements—such as creativity, experience, and coincidence—come into play. Nevertheless, skilled evaluators do not sit and wait for brilliant insight or lucky coincidence, they continue to probe, formulate, test, and adapt their ideas in an interactive manner to develop the most effective evaluation plan they can.

In this chapter, we will describe some of the elements of the interactive planning process that contribute to a viable evaluation plan. First, the notion of an evaluation plan will be discussed, so you will have an understanding of the ultimate objective of the focusing process. Then you will be introduced to a method for organizing client information to make it easier to formulate an evaluation plan. The evaluation information matrix will be used as an organizational tool to help you visualize the relationship between key types of information and bring practical evaluation tools to bear on the problems of the client. The process will be illustrated with examples based on the Midfield Preschool Program described in Chapter 3. The evaluation matrix is a useful organizational tool whether the evaluator is talking to an individual client or to a group of concerned people. However, groups can present additional problems that need to be considered. After describing the use of the matrix, there will be a brief description of techniques that can be used to help a group of individuals narrow the range of choices or reach a consensus. Finally, there will be a discussion of the problem of balancing the evaluator's point of view with the perspective of the client.

What Is an Evaluation Plan?

An evaluation plan is a framework that clarifies key elements of a proposed evaluation. There are three important topics that should be addressed in an evaluation plan:

(1) questions or issues to be examined by the evaluation,
(2) procedures to be employed in the evaluation, and
(3) resources needed to accomplish the evaluation tasks.

If the client and evaluator can agree on these general issues, they have set the stage for a formal agreement and a useful collaboration.

The evaluation plan need not be a formal written agreement; instead, it is usually an informal understanding derived from one or more focusing discussions. It will likely become the basis for subsequent written agreements or formal proposals. A verbal understanding such as the following will suffice in most circumstances.

> We are in general agreement about a six-month project to determine how many clients have been served in the adolescent substance-abuse program and how satisfied they are with the services. We will gather information from 100 to 150 past and present clients using questionnaires, and we will also conduct about two dozen telephone interviews and a dozen face-to-face interviews. The agency will help us organize an advisory committee of staff and clients to review the questionnaires and the interview protocols. The cost of these activities will be approximately $30,000. We will prepare a formal proposal with a detailed budget in a couple of weeks.

This is the sort of understanding you should strive to achieve. It indicates the general questions to be addressed and the kinds of procedures that will be employed. Approximate costs are described as well as the resources to be contributed by the client. It could easily form the basis for a formal written contract.

Though the plan is stated in very simple terms, it can result from a very complex series of discussions. Many meetings may be necessary to arrive at a clear understanding such as this. Nevertheless, the three elements—questions/concerns, procedures, and resources—should be specified in any evaluation plan.

A word of caution is in order at this point. Because the previous example was stated in such simple terms, you might be inclined to press for quick, simple agreements when you meet with a new client. This is generally not a good idea. You should take as much time as necessary to gather information and test out alternative strategies. Your first goal is to understand the program and the concerns of the client as well as possible. Only then can you formulate effective evaluation plans. You may discuss many problems before focusing on a small number of questions that are most important. You may think of many different techniques for collecting information before deciding on those that are most appropriate. We recommend that you try to get "all the cards on the table" so you can sort through them to produce the best hand.

Formulating a Plan

How do you develop an evaluation plan like the simple one we just described? It is a synthesis of the information you learned from the client and the knowledge of evaluation practices you already possess. In the plan you try to bring your expertise to bear on the concerns of the client. Formulating a plan is the process of combining these two elements. In Chapter 3 you learned how to gather information. From other books in the *Program Evaluation Kit* series as well as from your own training and experience you know about evaluation design, testing and measurement, qualitative techniques, and the other tools of an evaluator. In this chapter, we are going to talk about organizing the information you obtain about the program and the client's needs to make it easier to use your skills to develop solutions.

As you might imagine, this is an interactive process. You ask, the client answers. You sort through the client's descriptions, think about evaluation techniques, and propose activities. The client reacts to your suggestions, giving you more information. You readjust your tentative plans and ask additional questions. Out of this interchange you improve your ideas, establish priorities, clarify costs, and arrive at an acceptable

plan. The Midfield Preschool Program described in Chapter 3 provides
an illustration of how this might occur. We will summarize some of the
points described in Chapter 3 to provide a general example.

Example: The Midfield Preshool Program

Imagine that you are talking with Ms. Timms, the director of the Midfield
Preschool Program. She indicates that she wants an evaluation report to
share with parents and the local school board, but is not sure how to go
about conducting the evaluation herself. You begin by asking her to
describe the program. She tells you about their goals of helping the "at risk"
child through a modified Montessori approach. You help her expand the
description by asking specific questions about such things as the characteristics of the participants, the anticipated outcomes, the operation of the
program, and differences between sites. As she talks, you note evaluation-
related ideas that the conversation provokes in your own mind.

Once you have a clearer idea about the program's purposes and
procedures you ask Ms. Timms to clarify your understanding of the reasons
for the evaluation. You learn about the federal mandates as well as her
interest in obtaining data that would be useful to her and her staff. As is
often the case, she hopes to use the results of the evaluation to convince local
constituents of the value of the program. Of course, you cannot promise
that the results will be favorable, so you clarify your ethical responsibility to
conduct a fair and objective study. As the conversation continues, you begin
to make mental notes about those outcomes that could be measured
accurately and about techniques you could use to gather such information.
For example, follow-up data that could be used to track participants'
development after they leave the program may be available from the
district's records once the children enter kindergarten. Such data might
allow you to do a longitudinal analysis of program impact over time. With
this in mind, you ask additional questions about the kinds of records that
the district keeps and the variables they measure on a regular basis.

In this way, you begin to build and test tentative data-gathering and
analysis strategies that might meet the client's needs. You also learn about
some constraints, such as access to data, that may limit what you are able to
do. This activity continues as you focus on other possible questions and
think about other methods for obtaining and analyzing relevant data.

Ms. Timms encourages you to speak with other staff and parents, and
you learn about other concerns that might be addressed in an evaluation.
Ultimately, choices will have to be made, so you try to be sensitive to the
staff's priorities. Which issues are really of greatest interest to the director
and the constituents? Which are less important? While you are discussing
these priorities, you may also want to offer your own suggestions about
questions that can and cannot be measured reliably. For example, cognitive
development can be measured in a number of ways, but emotional
development is much more difficult to quantify.

Depending upon your approach to evaluation you might spend additional time talking about operationalizing variables, clarifying goals, involving program staff in the evaluation, seeking out the viewpoints of other interested groups, or understanding the decision-making process. Eventually, you organize your ideas into more complete evaluation strategies and share these with Ms. Timms. You also try to estimate their cost. Though these are only rough estimates, you will need to determine the resources necessary to carry out your plans and the value of these resources in dollars. Knowing approximately how much money Ms. Timms has to spend may affect the kinds of alternatives you propose.

It is hoped that after much discussion you will reach an agreement on an outline for the evaluation. You may decide to focus on two key questions, using existing records and observations of behavior for gathering data. Ms. Timms will pledge the staff's assistance in certain tasks, such as keeping additional records. You will estimate that the job can be done for about $6,000 which is somewhat higher than Ms. Timms wanted but may be acceptable. The meeting will end amiably, and you will return to your office to think things over and prepare a detailed proposal.

Although this description is somewhat abbreviated, it highlights many of the things that must take place for a successful collaboration to emerge. In most cases, the evaluator knows little about the program to start, and must think while learning. Even if evaluator and client have many meetings, with time in between for research and planning, the process involves the same steps. In the next section, we will present a system for organizing this process to help you develop better evaluation plans and offer more useful assistance to clients.

The Evaluation Information Matrix

We think of the process of formulating an evaluation plan as one of synthesizing ideas from two different sources. The first set of ideas are those you obtain from the client—the "what," "how," and "why" of the program. The second set are those you supply from your training and experience as an evaluator—ideas about data collection, analysis, and communication. When you devise a plan for an evaluation, you are bringing your skills to bear on the client's questions and concerns.

Your ability to make such a synthesis effectively depends on a number of things. First, it depends on the evaluation skills and abilities you possess. The more techniques you know, the more likely you will be to find an approach that will fit a given situation. These evaluation strategies are the kinds of things you may learn in a graduate program in evaluation, from books, or from direct experience. The other books in the *Program Evaluation Kit* are one good source of information about techniques you can apply to evaluation questions.

Second, your ability to be an effective evaluation planner depends on your skill at gathering information from clients and organizing it in a way that highlights evaluation-related issues and illuminates the connections between relevant facts. Doing this well will increase your success at bringing your own knowledge to bear on the client's concerns. Suggestions for gathering information were offered in Chapter 3. In this chapter, we will present a method for organizing these data that will make the task of developing strategies and formulating plans easier.

Third, your ability to synthesize depends on your own creativity. Each evaluation presents a unique set of circumstances which may require new solutions. While basic evaluation procedures can be applied directly to many situations, you will need to adapt techniques to fit many others. Sometimes you will create new approaches unlike any you have seen before. We cannot teach you to be creative, though we believe that creativity is enhanced by increased knowledge and experience.

The evaluation information matrix presented in Figure 1 is an organizational tool you can use for storing information and summarizing ideas during the planning process. Though it is presented in a written form, we think of it more as a mental tool, the kind of grid you would fill out "in your mind's eye" as you meet with a client. However, you may find that you prefer to take notes on paper using the evaluation information matrix as a guide. You should use whichever procedure works most effectively for you.

The six columns of the matrix represent the types of information you will need to construct a good evaluation plan. Some of these data will be supplied primarily by the client (including project components and objectives, questions and issues, and priorities) while some you supply yourself based on your own approach to evaluation and your knowledge of evaluation practices. The most important elements that you will provide are techniques for measuring variables, procedures for gathering information, and estimates of the resources needed to carry out the components of the plan.

While the process of formulating an evaluation plan rarely occurs in a perfectly linear manner, it is easiest to review the elements in the matrix from left to right. This orientation illuminates the logical relationships between the information contained in the columns.

The first column is for descriptive information, highlighting the

Program components (what?)	Issues/ questions (why?)	Constraints	Evaluation procedures	Priority	Costs/ resources

Figure 1. Evaluation information matrix

objectives and activities of each major program component. The second column provides a place to indicate the client's concerns regarding each component and record any specific questions to be answered. Such questions naturally lead to evaluation planning. However, before considering specific procedures, it is useful to note any obvious constraints that would limit the evaluator's options. Thus the third column is used to record special conditions that must be considered when developing procedures for addressing each concern.

Each of these columns is divided in half to provide space for noting evaluation-related thoughts and ideas that occur in response to information provided by the client. As information is provided by the client, it triggers ideas in the mind of the evaluator, these can be recorded in the second half of each column. These are not full-fledged designs or plans of attack; rather, they are notions about possible procedures or thoughts about strategies that later might go into the evaluation plan. So far most of the information has been provided by the client. In the fourth column, the evaluator responds by suggesting procedures for gathering and analyzing relevant information. These plans evolve from the ideas recorded in the previous three columns. Now, however, they are more fully developed and comprehensive. While formulating such plans, the evaluator may identify other constraints that can be added to the notes in the third column.

There are often more questions than the client can afford to have answered, so the fifth column provides a place to make notes about the client's priorities. Finally, the sixth column is used to record the evaluator's estimates of the cost of the alternatives that have been proposed. The evaluator can use the data in the last two columns to help the client balance priorities with costs and arrive at the best evaluation plan.

The use of the matrix will be described in greater detail in the next sections. We will refer to the Midfield Preschool Program described in Chapter 3 as an example of evaluation planning.

Program components (what?). The first step in formulating a plan is to obtain a clear understanding of the program, and the first column of the evaluation information matrix provides a place to make notes about key program elements. Chapter 3 described the kinds of questions you may want to ask to gather information about the program. During this conversation, the evaluator strives to understand each program component—how it operates and what it hopes to accomplish. As this information is obtained, the evaluator makes mental notes or records key phrases in the evaluation information matrix.

Figure 2 provides an example of the mental notes that might be made during the discussion of the Midfield Preschool Program described in Chapter 3. The evaluator has recorded information about the purposes of the program and the kinds of activities that take place. When evaluation-related ideas occurred these were noted in the second half of the column. Notice that these thoughts relate to all the various aspects of evaluation, including variable definition, data collection, treatment specification, data analysis, and communication of findings.

For the purpose of formulating a plan, you may want to organize your knowledge of the program into meaningful chunks, and think about developing the plan "componentwise"—that is, chunk by chunk. The size of these chunks will depend on both the nature of the program and your approach to evaluation. For example, a goal-oriented

Program Components (what?)

Population: "At risk" children develop- mental lag, but social independence voluntary participation in order of score	How do they measure these variables? Compare with nonselected group?
Purposes: Stimulation for social,* physical, cognitive development*	Observe social skills? Review their tests
Records: Continuum of skills	Pre-post comparison
Operation: small groups (8), half-day 4 sites: 1 teacher/1 aide (Blake Street different) 25 minutes group language 60 minutes Montessori play Snack 35 minutes cognitive skills *Indicates particular emphasis.	AM-PM differences? Site differences? Implementation analysis? Oral language test What impact?

Figure 2. Evaluation information matrix, with notes about components.

evaluator may want to distinguish as many different goal-directed activities as possible, while a responsive evaluator may prefer to think of the program as a single complex entity. These divisions will vary from situation to situation.

Question/issues (why?). In the next column, the evaluator notes the questions or concerns expressed by the client about each component. As noted in Chapter 3, program personnel may have very specific questions they want the evaluation to address ("Are students' reading scores improving now that they are using the Martin system?"); they may have broader concerns ("Are the neighborhood clinics working as well as they should be?"); or they may raise only very general issues ("Staff do not seem to be operating efficiently"). You should try to ascertain as many of the client's questions or concerns as possible.

Figure 3 illustrates the type of notes an evaluator might make in column 2 of the evaluation information matrix during the discussion of the Midfield Preschool Program. Again, the second half of the column has been used extensively to compile the evaluator's ideas in response.

Though this is the second column in our matrix, clients actually may begin the discussion by indicating the questions they want answered.

Issues/Questions (why)

Generate support	Study team?
parents	Board member involved
school board	Parents
Show effectiveness*	Their tests plus what else?
Prior: average # skills	
Mandated fund. agent	See last report, format
Outcomes:	
long term gains?	Follow-up data?
comparison group?	Not exactly matched, regression analysis?
Teacher:	
good rapport w/parents	Testimonials?
Use of aides?	Too time consuming
Ms. Applebee (teacher):	
parent involvement	Home interviews?
Montessori play?	What goals?
Ms. Lo (parent):	
good feelings	Parent questionnaire?
non-English communication*	What %?
*Indicates particular emphasis.	Parents/teachers lack insight, qualitative analysis?

Figure 3. Evaluation information matrix, with notes about issues/questions.

From their perspective, they are "getting right to the point," and this may be a very good sign. Clients with questions have done some thinking about their program and their needs for information. As an evaluator, you should not be surprised if you receive information about questions and issues before you have a very thorough understanding of the program. You need to be flexible enough to accept questions as a starting point and work backward to clarify your knowledge of the program.

For now, the form of the questions is not important. Your goal is to understand the client's needs clearly enough to begin to formulate procedures to address them. Depending on your approach to evaluation, you may want to have these questions restated in a particular form at some later point. For example, a goal-oriented evaluator may want to establish a clear connection between the evaluation questions and the program's stated goals and objectives. One of the activities he or she might suggest would be to clarify program objectives and evaluation criteria.

While you probably want to know enough about the entire program to understand how the elements fit together (column 1), you do not need to have questions about every component in the evaluation. Clients may be completely satisfied with some program components or they may have all the information they need to monitor these activities. You do not need to press for questions or problems relating to every program component. In fact, given the limited resources available for most evaluations, you probably will not be able to answer all the questions that are raised.

Constraints. By constraints, we mean special conditions or considerations that might limit your ability to carry out a procedure. For example, if you are called in to consult with a client after a program cycle has already begun, then it may not be possible to get baseline information reflecting participants' status at the start of the program. Thus you might not be able to measure growth accurately. In this case, the timing of the evaluation constrains what you can accomplish. As we discussed in Chapter 3 other constraints include such varied factors as scheduling conflicts within the program, regulations that require certain kinds of data collection, limited access to information (e.g., to preserve confidentiality), program guidelines that preclude certain kinds of comparisons (e.g., rules that require all participants to receive the same services so no control group can be used), and the willingness of program staff to participate in new data-gathering and reporting activities.

Of course, monetary constraints may be the most important of all. In most cases, there is only a certain amount of money that can be used for evaluation services, and the plan you propose must stay within certain budgetary limits. A separate column has been provided for estimating the cost of evaluation alternatives, but the clients fiscal limitation can be noted in the third column along with other constraints.

Figure 4 shows the kinds of notes you might make in the constraints column during the "what," "how," and "why" discussions of the Midfield Preschool Program. Once again, the column is divided in half to allow the evaluator to make brief notes about evaluation ideas that occur as constraints are noted.

Constraints usually emerge at two different points in your discussion

Constraints

< $5,000!	Few interviews, little qualitative work, use their staff a lot
Timeline:	
Full year,	OK for pre-post
March, for April Board	Need additional spring test
spring, for parents	
next fall, for teachers	
Good archives,	Longitudinal analysis
preschool developmental test	Check these instruments
oral language	„ „ „
skills test	„ „ „
teacher comments	
Participants and nonparticipants	Comparison group
? records,	Limited variables,
kindergarten standardized tests	Do they match preschool variables?
Secretarial support	Data-gathering from records
Teachers too	

Figure 4. Evaluation information matrix, with notes about constraints.

with a client. As just noted, you may learn about some constraints as you obtain your initial description of the program. If you are thinking ahead as you discuss the program's goals and activities you may learn things that will affect your later choices.

You may also uncover additional constraints as you develop strategies for conducting the evaluation. When you think about procedures for addressing the client's problems, be alert to any special conditions that will be necessary to carry out your plans. For example, if you are going to propose to conduct one-on-one interviews with clients to elicit firsthand impressions about an issue, you need to verify that it will be possible to find a time and place for such a conversation to occur. Alternatively, if you want to gather information from program staff about clients' attendance or participation, you will need to confirm the program administrator's willingness to have staff assume this task and the staff's willingness to do it accurately.

Limits on contributed resources are one of the most common constraints. There are a number of reasons why you may need the program administrators or staff to assume the responsibility for some tasks (to facilitate data collection, improve accuracy, reduce costs, etc.). These must always be reviewed with the client to ensure that they are able and willing to conduct these activities.

Evaluation procedures (measurement and design). This is the point at which your role shifts from the gatherer of information to the supplier of ideas. As we indicated at the beginning of this chapter, there should be a logical connection between what the program is designed to accomplish, how it operates, and how you propose to evaluate it. This is the point at which you formulate tentative evaluation strategies and make these connections clear for the client.

This is also the point at which any evaluation-related notes you made earlier in the conversation will come into play. It is from these kernels of ideas and your previous training and experience that the evaluation modules will evolve. At this stage you begin to formulate procedures for obtaining, interpreting, and reporting information to address the questions that have been identified and share these with the client.

The evaluation information matrix should help in this process. First, you should now have a clear understanding of the program elements and issues you outlined in the first three columns (or be able to point out instances in which connections are obscure). Second, your notes from the second half of columns one, two, and three contain bits of an evaluation plan which can be assembled into meaningful components.

Figure 5 provides an example of the kinds of activities an evaluator might propose to address the questions in the Midfield Preschool Program. Notice that more than one alternative has been developed for some questions. As you formulate solutions in your mind, you may think of many ways to address an issue. Eventually, one will be selected, but you should not reject others too quickly. You may want to share alternatives with the client, propose "trial balloons" to see if you have overlooked important factors that make one more desirable than another. If the choice is not clear, consider retaining multiple options. As you gather more information on constraints and think about resource demands, you will be able to select the best approach.

How do you figure out the elements of the evaluation plan? How do you think of procedures to address the client's concerns? Unfortunately, there are no simple answers to these questions. However, each module you propose will have to include three things: (1) a method for gathering information, (2) a plan for analyzing the information, and (3) a method for communicating. To be meaningful, these activities will have to relate to something the client has discussed, such as the program's goals, its

Evaluation Procedures

Form support/advisory team
  (to maximize impact)
    school board member
    parents
    teachers
    aides

Effectiveness:
  a. Pre-post gains (fall-spring):
    1. developmental (using their tests, if OK)
    2. cognitive skills (using their tests, if OK)
    3. social (observations?)
    4. physical (using data from archives, too)

  b. Longitudinal analysis:
    K-1-2 (cohort 1)
    K-1   (cohort 2)
    K   (cohort 3)

  c. Comparison group analyses:
    Non-admitted "at risk" vs. participants
      using screening tests and
      later kindergarten scores
      (regression discontinuity)

      using special program
      participation

Parent reports:
  questionnaire

Communication with and involvement of parents:
  open-ended interviews
  with parents (10) per site

  open-ended interviews
  with teachers (2) and aides (2)

Figure 5. Evaluation information matrix, with notes about procedures.

operation, or questions about it. In light of your approach and the client's need, you will propose datagathering strategies such as tests, observations, interviews, questionnaires, or document analysis. You will analyze the information quantitatively or qualitatively as is appropriate to the method you select, and you will report it in a manner that enhances its usefulness. This book is not designed to teach you about data collection, analysis, or reporting. Other books in this series provide this information. Our goal is to show you how various elements integrate into the overall process of focusing an evaluation. The evaluation information matrix can help in this focusing process by highlighting the key issues and important pieces of information. However, much of the synthesis must come from the evaluator. Some people begin by thinking about information: What information can you gather that relates to something in the program? Others begin by thinking about questions: What does the client want to know that you see a way to answer? You will have to find the approach that works best for you.

As you think about proposing evaluation strategies it may be useful to distinguish between issues of "measurement" and issues of "design." This distinction is clearest when you are answering questions about program impact. In this context, "measurement" refers to the process of obtaining a score or measure of some variable, while "design" refers to the schedule that is used for collecting scores and the comparisons that are made among scores to indicate the impact of the program over time.

For example, one of the issues in the Midfield Preschool Program is growth in children's physical development. Two problems must be solved to determine if such growth occurred. The first is a measurement problem: How do you quantify "physical development"? Surely it is more than just height and weight, but is it manual dexterity, balance, or something else? How do you measure it—with a timed agility test, with an observational checklist, or with other methods? Here the problem is developing a procedure to obtain a reliable indicator of this idea.

In many cases, the issue of measurement has already been addressed. For example, some programs have goals or objectives that specify the way variables are to be measured. In other cases, there is only one natural way to quantify a concept, such as "number of clients being served." In educational programs, many variables can be measured with existing tests, and the evaluator does not have to worry about developing new procedures. However, sometimes a new test needs to be constructed, and the evaluator needs to be prepared to do this. Beyond tests, many variables are best measured through interviews, questionnaires, observations, or reviews of existing documents and archival records. These are all tools the evaluator can use to gather data that will be meaningful to the client.

The evaluator who adopts a responsive approach is extremely concerned about the questions of measurement. However, he or she deals with it in a very different way. In order to capture subtle differences and be more sensitive, the responsive evaluator adopts qualitative techniques that deemphasize counting and simplifying observations. The responsive evaluator rejects pressures to summarize variables in a single score, preferring more complex descriptions that contain as much richness and detail as possible.

Once the question of measurement is solved, a second issue must be addressed: How do you determine if the program produced changes in the variable you measured? Surely you will need more than one measurement on each child, but will it be sufficient to measure each child at the start and at the end of the program or will you need more frequent measurements? How will you determine if the changes are due to the program rather than just natural maturation or other activities that were happening outside the preschool? This is the question of design. The problem is quantifying changes over time and determining whether they were attributable to the program or to other extraneous influences.

So, in addition to selecting a measurement strategy that is appropriate, you may also need to think about a research design that will allow you to determine the relationship between program activities and their effects. A research design is a set of procedures for organizing the collection and comparison of data to ensure that the conclusions that are drawn are valid. For example, a familiar design involves randomly assigning participants to groups that receive different treatments, collecting data at two points in time (usually at the beginning and end of some program treatment), and using the changes over time as an indicator of the impact of the treatments. Such designs are additional tools the evaluator uses to address client's concerns. Evaluators who adopt an experimental approach place the greatest emphasis on maintaining the integrity of the design as an assurance of the validity of the conclusions, but other evaluators rely upon designs as well.

Priorities. One thing will be true in almost every evaluation negotiation: There will not be sufficient resources to answer all the questions that emerge from a thorough discussion of the program. This fact must be considered when formulating an evaluation plan. Because there are not enough resources to address all the interesting issues, the client will have to make choices. Though the final decision belongs to the client, the evaluator has a strong influence on this decision. To offer more appropriate advice, the evaluator needs to know the client's priorities. Consequently, you should make an effort to determine which issues are of greatest importance to the client.

Most likely the most important questions will be those that are raised first, but this is not always the case. If you are able to conduct a broad, wide-ranging conversation about the program, you may find that deeper, more fundamental questions emerge later in the discussion. Another clue that an issue is important is that the client returns to it again and again during the conversation.

However, do not assume that the topics mentioned first or returned to most often are, in fact, the most important without checking on this. Frequently, clients have very limited conceptions of evaluation and ask very simple questions because they do not realize that more complex issues can be addressed. Do not take a statement such as "We want you to find out how much our students have gained since the beginning of the year" at face value. Find out if the person might, in fact, desire something very different if he or she knew it were possible. Through direct and indirect means you should try to determine which questions have the greatest importance for the client and note that in the matrix.

Figure 6 shows how the evaluation information matrix might appear after notes are made about priorities. We find that it is usually sufficient to classify questions into three categories representing high, medium, and low priorities. In Figure 6 the evaluator coded these with the letters H, M, and L; however, you can use any system you like. One alternative that some people prefer is to rank the questions in priority order from highest to lowest.

Before concluding this discussion, we need to emphasize that the problem of choosing which evaluation activities to undertake requires more than just determining the client's priorities and reflecting them in the evaluation plan. Two factors come into play when choosing among alternative evaluation activities. First, as just noted, some questions are more important to the client than others. A conscientious evaluator tries to establish the client's priorities and take them into account when formulating evaluation strategies.

Second, some questions can be more easily, more reliably, or more economically answered than others. For example, the client may place a great deal of importance on measuring changes in self-concept, but this is neither easily nor reliably done. It may cost more than the client is willing to pay, require so much time that it is disruptive to the program, or provide results that are not very reliable. In the final decision these factors may outweigh the clients initial priorities.

Cost. The final column in the information matrix is one of the most difficult to complete. Here you try to estimate the costs of the alternatives you are developing. Notice that we used the word "estimate,"

Evaluation Procedures	*Priorities*
Form support/advisory team	H
(to maximize impact)	
school board member	
parents	
teachers	
aides	
Effectiveness:	
a. Pre-post gains (fall-spring):	M
1. developmental (using their tests, if OK)	M
2. cognitive skills (using their tests, if OK)	M
3. social (observations?)	M
4. physical (using data from archives, too)	L
b. Longitudinal analysis:	
K-1-2 (cohort 1)	
K-1 (cohort 2)	
K (cohort 3)	
c. Comparison group analyses:	
Non-admitted "at risk" vs. participants	
using screening tests and	H
later kindergarten scores	
(regression discontinuity)	
using special program	H
participation	
Parent reports:	L
questionnaire	
Communication with and involvement of parents:	
open-ended interviews	
with parents (10) per site	L
open-ended interviews	L
with teachers (2) and aides (2)	

Figure 6. Evaluation information matrix, with notes about priorities

not "calculate." At this time all you are trying to do is determine a rough estimate, a "ballpark figure," to approximate the expense involved in carrying out each alternative. Later, when you are preparing a written agreement, you will prepare a detailed budget with accurate cost figures.

Figure 7 shows the cost estimates made during the discussion of the

Evaluation Procedures	Priorities	Resources/Cost
Form support/advisory team (to maximize impact) school board member parents teachers aides	H	District staff time (15 hours contributed) Parent time ($5/hour?) Evaluator (15 hours) $750

Effectiveness:
a. Pre-post gains (fall-spring):
  1. developmental
  2. cognitive skills
  3. social (observations?)
  4. physical
  (using data from archives, too)
	
	M
	M
	M
	M
	L
		Data collection
		(30 hours contributed)
		(omit observations)
		Research analyst
		(40 hours) $800
		Evaluator (10 hours) $500

b. Longitudinal analysis:
  K-1-2 (cohort 1)
  K-1   (cohort 2)
  K   (cohort 3)
		Data collection
		(50 hours contributed)
		Research analyst
		(40 hours) $800
		Evaluator (10 hours) $500

c. Comparison group analysis:
  Non-admitted "at risk" vs. participants
    using screening tests and
    later kindergarten scores
    (regression discontinuity)
	
	H
		Data collection
		(20 hours contributed)
		Research associate
		(10 hours) $250
		Computer time $100

using special program participation	H	Data collection (45 hours contributed) Research analyst (10 hours) $200
Parent reports: questionnaire	 L	Evaluator (10 hours) $500 Research analyst (20 hours) $400

Communication with and involvement
of parents:
  open-ended interviews
  with parents (10) per site
	
	L
		
		Research associate
		(20 hours) $500
		Evaluator (20 hours) $1000

open-ended interviews with teachers (2) and aides (2)	L	Evaluator (10 hours) $500
		General clerical support (50 hours) $400
		$8000

Figure 7. Evaluation information matrix, with cost estimates

Midfield Preschool Program. Notice that they are all rounded off to the nearest hundred dollars. This makes the estimation process easier, and reinforces for the client the fact that the amounts are not exact.

It is very difficult for us to provide any dollar figures you could use for estimating costs. By the time you read this book, inflation will have changed the costs of most of the goods and services that would be part of an evaluation. Moreover, the cost of the same services varies from location to location, so our California estimates might be inappropriate for your city or town.

Instead of suggesting actual numbers, we can suggest a procedure for carrying out this exercise. The method we prefer subdivides the process into two steps: (1) determining the resources needed, and (2) estimating the cost in dollars of each resource. To estimate costs in this manner, you begin by specifying all the things you will need to carry out the evaluation. This includes the number of professional staff and the amount of time each will put into the activity; the materials that will be needed (such as tests); the number of support staff that will be needed for typing, coding, and sorting duties, and how much time will be required of each; the necessary travel; the amount of mailing, duplicating, and printing required; any services you intend to contract out to others, such as machine scoring of tests; and other miscellaneous activities.

Once this list is completed, you assign dollar costs to each category and compute the total. These costs are based on the prevailing wage rates and prices at the time of the evaluation. If these figures have changed by the time you plan your next evaluation you can adjust the multipliers you apply to each resource. The process of determining the necessary resources remains the same. Levin (1985) is an excellent guide for estimating evaluation costs.

Working with groups. To this point clients have been portrayed as individuals; this was done to simplify the discussion and emphasize the focusing processes. However, in many situations the evaluator will have to work with a group of concerned people rather than a single individual. Even when the initial discussions are conducted with a single sponsor, larger numbers of constituents may be brought into the process at key points at the request of the client or the evaluator. Consequently, the evaluator needs to be familiar with techniques for helping groups discuss an issue and reach consensus.

As a starting point, three popular techniques for working with groups will be described. The techniques will be presented as they might be used to help a group establish priorities for an evaluation. This is the stage at which larger groups are most often consulted to ensure that all significant constituencies have input into the evaluation process. Setting priorities is often a group decision-making process. Several individuals may need to be involved in determining which questions are most important to address, whether the individuals represent different roles within the same organization, or different organizations with a stake in the same program. When a group is involved, the problem of setting priorities is more complex than it is with a single client, since individuals occupying different organizational positions are likely to bring very different values, perspectives, and information needs to the process.

The evaluator may wish to hold a meeting of the evaluation clients to determine the priorities for the evaluation. This reduces the risk of misunderstanding or distrust which can result if the evaluator attempts to work with several clients individually, and is likely to result in more widespread interest and acceptance of the results. The approach is not without risk, however. Frustration and confusion may result if the group is leaderless or fails to agree upon its task and a process for accomplishing it.

The evaluator often assumes the role of group facilitator. The facilitator does not necessarily lead or chair the group, but helps it to move efficiently toward establishing priorities. He or she explains the task facing the group, and suggests a process or a menu of processes for accomplishing the task. Once a process has been agreed upon, the facilitator keeps the group on track until the task is complete. To learn more about the role of a group facilitator, you may wish to read Doyle and Strauss (1976).

Several processes are available to facilitate group priority setting. Many consensus-building approaches share a common set of steps: (a) identifying options; (b) determining pros and cons, or costs and benefits, (c) proposing a solution, or ranking, with something for everyone, and (d) adjustments to achieve consensus or acceptance. For example, the process of assigning priorities to a list of evaluation questions might begin with the evaluator displaying the list of questions generated and asking for additions. After any additions have been made, each question is reviewed briefly, with group participants given an opportunity to explain why the question is or is not important to them. After each question has been addressed, participants individually rank each one on paper, adding a star next to the one or two questions they feel most essential, and a minus next to any question they feel definitely should *not* be addressed.

The evaluator tallies the responses in front of the group and circles a few (the number depending on the resources of the evaluation) emerging as priorities. To the extent possible, he or she avoids questions with minuses, and includes as many as possible with stars. The group then responds to this outcome, and the evaluator makes adjustments to try to eliminate any strong expressions of dissatisfaction. Ultimately, a final group ranking of the circled questions is proposed and is similarly adjusted.

More formal techniques may be required when dealing with large groups, strongly opposing viewpoints, or extremely long lists of options. Three such techniques—the Q-sort, the Delphi technique, and the nominal group approach—are described in Appendix A.

Evaluation approach. To this point, little has been said about the effect of the evaluator's approach on the planning process. Does a goal-oriented evaluator formulate a plan in the same manner as a decision-oriented evaluator? To a great extent the answer is yes; they go through the same process. Regardless of approach, the evaluator will need to know about the program and the client's concerns. Similarly, he or she will suggest strategies for answering questions and be concerned about constraints that might exist. All evaluators must deal with costs, too. As a result, the evaluation information matrix provides an organizational tool that is useful no matter which approach the evaluator adopts.

Instead, the emphasis of the evaluator will be seen in the information that is entered into the matrix (not the shell that is used to organize it). As you might imagine, the greatest differences between evaluators who adopt different approaches will be evident in the evaluation procedures that each proposes. However, differences may also be seen in the kinds of issues and concerns that are elicited. As we noted in Chapter 3, at a certain point an experimental evaluator may ask different questions than a user-focused evaluator or a responsive evaluator, and as a result may develop a different impression of the program and a different sense of the issues that are important to the client.

For most of us these differences are easily accommodated in the evaluation information matrix we have described. However, you may find that there are other things you want to record that do not fit into the matrix. Each evaluation approach emphasizes something slightly different, and these unique elements are important. For example, a user-oriented evaluator may want to take note of the likely information users. A decision-focused evaluation will need to capture information about important decision points in the future as the program develops. A responsive evaluator will want to compile a list of all the groups that have a stake in the outcome of the evaluation. These data are not afterthoughts, they are necessary information so each evaluator can develop an effective strategy. In a sense, they are all elements of the program and can be recorded in the first column of the matrix. However, you may find it easier to add additional space between columns two and three for recording such approach-specific information.

Selecting an approach. The final question you will have to answer is which approach should you use? Clearly, if there were only one answer to this question there would be no need to discuss five different approaches. As you might imagine, different evaluators believe in the efficacy of different approaches. We like to think of ourselves as eclectic evaluators, picking and choosing among approaches depending upon the situation, and this is the strategy we would recommend. Use the techniques that allow you to provide the client with the most useful and meaningful information. We believe this is the best course of action.

Negotiating an evaluation plan (choosing among alternatives). As we noted above, there are many different ways to do an evaluation, and the process of developing a plan in conjunction with the client is a process of choosing among alternatives. In many cases, you will have suggested specific evaluation activities throughout the discussion. Such testing of strategies is a good tactic that promotes meaningful dialogue and provides information you need to make better recommendations at later stages of the conversation. However, it is unlikely you will have made many firm decisions until you finish gathering information.

Once you have elaborated a matrix full of options, it is time to try to negotiate an agreeable evaluation plan. The two factors that will influence the choices the most are the client's priorities for information and the cost of the alternatives. Of course, many other factors, such as feasibility and reliability, come into play. However, because priorities and costs are so important they offer a good place to begin when discussing an actual plan.

One approach is for the evaluator to take the lead and propose a specific set of activities. Begin with those judged to be most important and continue until you are pretty sure that funds are exhausted. This becomes the initial plan for starting the negotiations. You might say, "For roughly $50,000 we could do the following things" or "To tell you everything you want to know might cost $20,000, on the other hand, for $10,000 we can answer X, Y, and Z." In one form or another, you want to offer a tentative package. Then you can begin to talk about details. As the client asks questions, you can explain why you suggested certain things. If the client wants more, you can discuss the cost. By this point, it should not be difficult to make adjustments to satisfy both the client's needs and the program's budget. If things go well, client and evaluator will be able to agree upon an evaluation plan that is both relevant and practical. Remember your goal: a general understanding that specifies questions, procedures, and costs.

Balancing evaluator's approach and client's expectations. Until now, we have assumed that you will be able to reach a comfortable compromise between your approach to evaluation and the client's expectations. This is a reasonable assumption in the vast majority of cases. Clients are looking to evaluators to provide expertise, and they are willing to listen to the advice that is offered.

Evaluators, too, are generally reasonable people. They try to offer advice that is appropriate for each situation. Rarely would a competent evaluator propose an approach that is contrary to the needs of the client. Instead, most evaluators are eclectic in their approach to evaluation, choosing one model or another as the situation warrants.

However, this is not always the case. Some evaluators believe quite firmly in one particular approach to evaluation. They would rather not undertake a project than do it in a manner that is not personally satisfying. If you feel strongly about one perspective toward evaluation, then you may have to exercise this option occasionally. You may politely decline to collaborate with a client if you are uncomfortable providing the services the client seems to want or need. You may try to enlighten the client about the benefits to be gained from adopting your approach. However, this should be done cautiously; it would be unethical to coerce a client or to produce an evaluation that fails to meet realistic needs.

Some clients have equally strong feelings about evaluation, and they may reject the ideas suggested by the evaluator. Sometimes this occurs because of a misunderstanding: A client familiar with one approach to evaluation may believe that this is the "proper" approach, or an evaluator may misunderstand the demands being placed on the client by constituents or regulations and so may propose truly unresponsive solutions. On rare occasions, there is a genuine incompatibility that cannot be resolved. In such circumstances the client, too, has the right to end the collaboration during the planning stage.

Of course, we assume that such circumstances will rarely come to pass. We hope that you can explain your beliefs well enough for a client to see their merit. We also hope that you have learned enough about focusing an evaluation to be able to obtain an accurate impression of the program and propose practical and relevant strategies for analysis. An evaluator who can ask effective questions, listen attentively, organize information, and formulate responsive plans should be able to satisfy the needs of most any client.

Appendix A
Techniques for Working with Groups

The Delphi technique, the Q-sort, and the nominal group technique are popular techniques for assisting groups to arrive at a decision. They may aid in focusing evaluations when several individuals or groups are involved in selecting among several options.

Delphi Technique

The Delphi technique, named for the Oracle at Delphi who predicted the future, was developed at the Rand Corporation starting in 1948. It began as an attempt to elicit a consensus of expert opinion regarding the future consequences of policies or trends. It is applicable as a tool for developing consensus generally, without a meeting of participants.

The Delphi technique employs written questionnaires with cycles of feedback rather than face-to-face discussion. Generally, each participant is asked to rate or rank individual options according to a numerical scale and to provide a written explanation for his or her ratings. These are then collected and aggregated. In the next iteration, each participant receives his or her original questionnaire, along with the anonymous, aggregated responses of the other participants and their comments. Participants are then asked to respond again, revising their original responses in light of others' responses, and providing written justification when they choose to differ from the group. The procedure is repeated to the point of consensus or diminishing returns.

The actual Delphi technique is generally applied when participants are unable to meet together. However, the general notion of cycling between individual ratings and group aggregate ratings as a means of reducing variation is commonly applied in groups.

Q-Sort

The Q-sort is a general sorting technique which can be applied whenever a large number of items need to be grouped or rated.

A list of items (evaluation questions, say) is generated, and each item is printed onto a 5" × 8" card. Cards are shuffled, and then numbered. Duplicate decks, identically numbered, may be produced. Each individual is then given instructions to sort the cards into piles according to some criterion. The instructions may be highly structured ("Sort the 40 cards into five levels of importance, with no more than 4 cards in the category of most importance") or less structured.

The Q-sort may be adapted to a group activity to achieve consensus on the sorting of items. One approach is to employ arithmetically expanding groups. First, participants sort in pairs and record their outcome. Pairs then combine into groups of four and are asked to identify the differences in their two versions and resolve them. Groups of four are then merged into groups of eight, and so on, until a single assignment of items is achieved by the entire group.

Nominal Group Technique

The nominal group technique is a process for leading a group to identify several options and to select among them. It works best with small groups of five to nine people.

The process generally involves five steps. First, group members work individually to generate lists of options in response to a question or a problem. Second, the facilitator leads the group in a round-robin listing of options until the complete set is before the group. This is followed by a controlled discussion in which options are clarified. Questions may be asked, but attacks or advocacy regarding particular options is discouraged. Individuals then rank the options individually or express preferences in a vote. Votes or rankings are tallied and displayed. In the final step the group discusses the options again in light of the vote tally. If necessary, participants vote again until a single option or sufficiently narrow range of options emerges.

The use of controlled discussion and voting in the nominal group technique is often effective in moving groups to a speedy decision if members are willing to accept the rule. However, the discouragement of debate may prevent a full discussion of the consequences of options and does not necessarily promote the selection of the best ones.

For more information about these methods consult Delbecq, Van de Ven, and Gustafson (1975) and Sanders and Cunningham (1974).

References

Alkin, M. C. (1969). Evaluation theory development. *Evaluation Comment, 2*(1), 1-4.

Alkin, M. C., Daillak, K., & White, P. (1979). *Using evaluations: Does evaluation make a difference?* Newbury Park, CA: Sage.

Braskamp, L. A., & Brown, R. D. (1980). *New directions for program evaluation: Utilization of evaluation information.* San Francisco: Jossey-Bass.

Campbell, D. T., & Stanley, J. C. (1966). *Experimental and quasi-experimental designs for research.* Chicago: Rand McNally.

Delbecq, A. L., Van de Ven, A. H., & Gustafson, D. H. (1975). *Group techniques for program planning.* New York: Scott Foresman.

Doyle, M., & Straus, D. (1976). *How to make meetings work.* New York: Wyden Books.

Lincoln, Y. S., & Guba, E. G. (1985). *Naturalistic inquiry.* Newbury Park, CA: Sage.

Levin, H. (1985). *Cost effectiveness: A primer.* Newbury Park, CA: Sage.

Patton, M. Q. (1986). *Utilization-focused evaluation.* Newbury Park, CA: Sage.

Popham, W. J. (1975). *Educational evaluation.* Englewood Cliffs, NJ: Prentice-Hall.

Popham, W. J. (1981). *Modern educational measurement.* Englewood Cliffs, NJ: Prentice-Hall.

Rossi, P. H., & Freeman, H. E. (1982). *Evaluation: A systematic approach.* Newbury Park, CA: Sage.

Sanders, J., & Cunningham, S. (1974). Techniques for formative evaluation. In G. Borich (Ed.), *Evaluation educational products.* Englewood Cliffs, NJ: Educational Technology Press.

Stake, R. E. (1975). *Evaluating the arts in education: A responsive approach.* Columbus, OH: Charles E. Merrill.

Stufflebeam, D. L., Foley, W. J., Gephart, W. J., Guba, E. G., Hammond, R. L., Merriman, H. O., & Provus, M. M. (1971). *Educational evaluation and decision making.* Itasca, IL: Peacock.

Index

NOTES

NOTES